PURVEYORS OF
HOPE
AND
GREENWOOD
SPLENDID GOODS ®

MISS HOPE'S
TEATIME
TREATS

1 3 5 7 9 10 8 6 4 2

Published in 2012 by Ebury Press, an imprint of Ebury Publishing

A Random House Group Company

The Random House Group Limited Reg. No. 954009

Addresses for companies within the Random House Group can be found at
www.randomhouse.co.uk

A CIP catalogue record for this book is available from the British Library

MIX
Paper from
responsible sources
FSC® C008047

The Random House Group Limited supports The Forest Stewardship
Council®(FSC®), the leading international forest certification organisation.
Our books carrying the FSC label are printed on FSC® certified paper.
FSC is the only forest certification scheme endorsed by the leading
environmental organisations, including Greenpeace. Our paper procurement
policy can be found at www.randomhouse.co.uk/environment

To buy books by your favourite authors and register for offers visit
www.randomhouse.co.uk

Printed and bound in China by C&C Offset Printing Ltd.

Every effort has been made to contact the copyright holders. Please contact
the publishers with any queries. Please note that conversions to imperial
weights and measures are suitable equivalents and not exact.

Design: Smith & Gilmour
Photography: Cristian Barnett
Styling: Miss Hope
Food styling: Emma Marsden

ISBN 9780091946654

For my Lickle Marmi –
for coddled eggs, hostess
trolleys, Georgina haircuts,
butter curls, duchess
potatoes and TBB2.

CONTENTS

HOPE AND GREENWOOD AT YOUR SERVICE

Hope and Greenwood are two frightfully nice people who like sweets. Miss Hope (that which is *moi*) has cherry-red lips, strawberry-blond hair, magnificent jellies and is a right handful. Mr G does not have a boat but he would like one, he has a captain's hat and a cork key fob. He enjoys piping Miss Hope onboard. He quaffs a good Rioja and murders a bacon banjo. He is follically challenged but makes up for this by having an admirable chest rug like a were-hamster.

I met Mr G at a dinner party round the corner, over a beetroot consommé and a baked Alaska, before you were born. Love sent thunderbolts and lightning; cherubs sang. One Hawaiian wedding later and we were united eternally in domestic, sweet-sucking bliss. Sometimes we hate each other and fight like strumpets at a shoe sale but most of the time I strop about in unsuitable heels whilst Mr G makes a nice cup of tea. Ying and yang, Abbot and Costello, Mary, Mungo and Midge (we don't talk about Midge).

And so we trundle forward to 2004 when I said the immortal words, 'You are lying on my hair,' closely followed by 'Where have all the sweet shops gone?' Thus it was that, snuggling under the duvet, we hatched a plan to bring the finest British confections into every pantry in Britain.

Very soon we opened our first sweet shop in a super place called East Dulwich in the 'burbs of London. Never contented, we popped out another one in Covent Garden in the star-sprinkled shadow of the Theatre Royal, Drury Lane. Very soon lots of nice people came along and said, 'Give us your sweets or else', and H&G spread its love into all the top-notch department stores and delightful delis in the land. After no sleep for seven years we opened some sweet shops in Japan. That was pretty clever, as it happens.

LADIES' AFTERNOON TEA

As a child, I was lucky enough to have a mother. You can call her Granny Hope; I will call her Lickle Marmi. I still have her. No amount of jostling near stairs or out-of-date lasagne will get her to yield my inheritance.

My Marmi was well versed in the manners of polite society, having gone to University in 1943. She knows what to do if your hem gets hitched in your knickers in church, how to summon a policeman with a monogrammed hankie and, most importantly how to stage Ladies' Afternoon Tea.

Many of the recipes in my book are inspired by, are an homage to, or indeed are blatantly stolen from my Marmi, such as Pear and Chocolate Trifle, Cucumber Sandwiches with Strawberry and Mint, Brandy Snaps with Spiced Mandarin Cream and Hazelnut Tarts with Strawberries. If you give her a call on her telephone she will advise you to have a proper teapot, silver, if possible, sugar tongs and good china. Strawberry fans and celery tassels are de rigueur and rainbow sugar is

a joy if you can find it. She will also tell you not to trust a man who walks like a cat.

I've spent the entire summer eating copious amounts of Honeycomb Meringues with Strawberries, Sticky Toffee and Ginger Cake, Petticoat Tails with Lavender and Honey, Asparagus and Prosciutto Lilies, Fig and Pecorino Crescia and Curried Egg Bridge Rolls with Pea Shoots: all this I have done for you at no extra cost. Naturally, eating is thirsty work and I succumbed to some Prosecco with Nasturtiums, Darjeeling Gin Fizz and Sicilian Lemonade. June, July and August were thus a blur, and by September I was in rehab.

So let us crack on, chums, the sunny morning marches on; the clock will soon strike three and is there honey still for tea? Starch your napkins and warm the pot. There is pastry to cook and buns to warm, eggs to chop and cucumbers to peel. Stand to attention, whisks at the ready, spatulas cocked.

Top-notch. Carry on.

LET'S HAVE A CUPPA

Afternoon Tea was invented (allegedly) by Anna, Duchess of Bedford, in the early 1800s. It transpires that she was a bit greedy and needed a savoury finger to fill a yawning gap. The Earl of Sandwich had already slapped his meat between two slices of bread and spawned the sarnie, thus the stage was set.

Some things to know about tea (in the order that my brain remembers them, i.e. random).

High tea is served on a high table or dinner table by hobbledehoys, wasters and scumbags at 6 o' clock. High tea or just 'tea' replaces dinner entirely. Avoid at all cost unless you have tracky bottoms.

Afternoon tea is served by posh folk on a low table at 4 o' clock – it's a standalone treat rather than a replacement meal.

Tee total: tea was used to replace the nation's favourite drink – gin. Not in my house.

China: teapots were designed in the style of Chinese wine bottles – thus 'china' tea services.

Volume: teatime treats should take the form of dainty morsels. Please eat twice as much.

Dancing: tea dances were most popular in Blighty during war time. If you care to cut a rug then Thriller and Ah-Ah-Ah Ah Stayin' Alive would be my preferences for a jolly good knees-up.

Tarts: In the mid-nineteenth century, ladies were allowed to go to tearooms unchaperoned. They were therefore not mistaken for prostitutes. Where's the fun in that?

Nutters: Bhismadeb Sarkar from Katwa, India, drank only tea for 22 years after his wife served his lunch a bit late. He vowed never to eat again to punish her. Whatever.

Geography: the town of Tea in South Dakota counts Annabelle's Adult Super Center among its major attractions.

Boston Tea Party: in 1773 there was a party in Boston on a boat. Some tea was chucked into the sea. I couldn't be bothered to read the rest.

Faux tea: tea made out of herbs, flowers or walrus scrapings is not tea.

Tea bagging: A New Yorker called Thomas Sullivan invented tea bagging. Shipping tea in tins was mega expensive so he wrapped the tea in a gauze packet. His American customers dunked the whole bag in the pot and thus, by happy accident, the teabag was invented.

Beauty: a damp tea bag placed on a closed eyelid will refresh your teddy tired eyes; brunettes will add shine to their locks by rinsing them in tea. A brunette with tired eyes should stay home and not go carousing on a school night.

Tasseography is the art of fortune telling by reading symbols in tea leaves. If you see an apple expect a pat on the back; flying birds bring good news; a candle symbolises enlightenment; a cat is a lying friend; a dog is a loyal friend; a raven is bad news; and a burly man with rippling muscles and tight buns waving a heart-shaped sign upon which is inscribed your name is in fact gay.

How to make a proper cuppa
Keep your tea in an airtight container.
Use freshly boiling water.
Warm the [damn] teapot.
One spoonful of tea per person and one for the pot.
Give the tea five minutes to draw.
Stir the brew once.
Milk; for or aft.
Thank you.

(As 96% of all cups of tea drunk daily in the UK are brewed from tea bags I suggest you dunk a bag and waggle it about like a builder.)

THE ETIQUETTE OF AFTERNOON TEA

My dear Miss Hope (and Monty),

Thank you for the delightful afternoon we spent at Westbury Square. It was delicious to see you.

I must, my dear, take a moment to congratulate you on your afternoon tea table and, forgive me, while we have come a long way to civilise Monty, he has still so much to learn about manners.

Thank you ever so for the stiffy invitation, it's such a thrill to trot down to breakfast and see a proper invitation card on the silver tray in the hall. I called Frederick immediately to prepare the carriage and young Rose laid out my white dress with baby blue ribbons in preparation.

Your afternoon tea table, Miss Hope, was, as ever, laden with the finest treats; a slice of the best homemade cake here, beautifully crisp biscuits there. Your Cherry Genoa Cake, Squirrel Greenwood's Fruit Cake and Lavender Petticoat Tails tickled my fancy. And, oh my, the delicate pastries, bite-sized but plentiful. I confess, I ate twice as much as my corsetry would allow.

You are quite correct to assume that four o'clock is, and always will be, the most suitable hour for taking tea, and you do it so ardently. Your best linen tablecloth and napkins, starched and pressed, your finest china, the silver teapot, cake forks and bone-handled cutlery are such a joy, dear lady. How smart Monty looked! I noted his starched collar and the glint of the gold buttons on his red waistcoat. But I wonder if he really needed 32 sugar cubes in his tea? It took me all my time not to thwack him with the sugar tongs.

I'm delighted to see that Monty is at the very least trying to master the art of tea-making; so essential for polite society, don't you think? I noted with great pleasure that he took care to fetch the best china teapot and warm it first with boiling water, leaving it to heat up for a minute or two, no more, no less. I was less impressed when he emptied the water into the aspidistra, but heartened by his keen measuring of tea leaves – one teaspoonful per person, plus one for the pot – topped up with freshly boiled water. Alas, I did feel Monty's impatience as he waited the full three minutes for the tea to brew. Pulling faces will not do. I have only a very few splashes on my muslin gown and I'm sure Rose will be able to scrub them out on my return to Crasters.

Still, it was a pleasure to watch Monty deftly arranging the cakes and treats in the middle of the table on a splendid variety of plates and cake stands. Please do not worry yourself about the broken glass; Harley Street is a mere 10 minutes away, even with a limp.

I must also congratulate you, Miss Hope, as I noted that Monty has been paying attention: he poured the milk into his teacup first and his teacup was never very far from its saucer. Bless him, he even held the handle with the thumb and forefinger of one hand, with the saucer hovering just underneath as a nearby platform. I had never noticed, however, how hairy Monty's hands are, and it quite made me shudder. I fear we may need to fetch the barber!

Thank you again, dear lady, and I look forward to seeing you at Crasters for tea in the near future. In the meantime perhaps you could have a word with Monty about sitting on the table? We have chairs at Crasters for this very purpose. I'm very sorry to hear that the chandelier is irreplaceable; too much swinging perhaps?

Kindest regards to you and your monkey,

Miss Elizabeth Bonnet

PS Please ask Monty not to press his person against the drawing room window – it scares the horses.

TARTING IT UP

If you fancy tarting up your splendid teatime treats, here is a list of smashing edible nonsenses. Please flip to page 125 and take a gander. Many of them were whittled and tweaked by my sister and me for my mum's luxury Demis Roussos parties.

CELERY FANCIES

Avail yourself of two sticks of celery and cut them to 10cm lengths. Place the celery vertically on a board. Holding the sticks firmly at the top, put your knife in one of the ridges 3cm from the top and cut all the way down to the board. Continue to cut through and down the ridges at about 2mm intervals along the width of each piece of celery to cut it into long tassles, making sure each stick remains intact at the top. Place them in a bowl of iced water overnight and the tassles will fan out. They'll absorb a lot of water, so drain well on kitchen paper before serving. You can use the same technique on spring onions, too, no expense spared.

CUCUMBER TWISTS

Trim one end from a cucumber, and thinly slice around a quarter of it into rounds using a sharp knife. To make a twist, cut one straight line from the middle of a slice to the edge, then hold the two open edges and pull them away from each other, akimbo. Place them on the plate. If you have no life you may wish to do two together for more impact.

TOMATO LILIES

Choose small firm tomatoes for these, but not cherry tomatoes. Take a small sharp paring knife and push it into the middle of the tomato, at a slight angle. Cut around the middle of the tomato in a zig-zag shape. Separate the two halves to make two tomato lilies. Look at you.

COURGETTE TASSLES

This is best done on a small courgette; size is everything. Trim the ends from the top and bottom of a courgette. Slice strips, a couple of millimetres thick, along the length of the courgette. Lay the strips on a board so they're lying horizontally along it. Leaving the top 5mm of the length of each strip as the border, cut vertically down the width of each strip to make little tassles. Roll up each slice of courgette, securing the uncut border with a little piece of cocktail stick. The little strips will fan out like a tassle. Very burlesque.

RADISH TOADSTOOLS

Choose big radishes for these, otherwise this is really fiddly. Trim the leaves, stem and root, and score the equator of the radish with a small sharp knife, cutting about halfway in, but not all the way through. Slice from the stem end at a right angle into the radish until you reach the horizontal cut. Turn and repeat the slice four times, leaving a square at the stem end, so you're left with a white stubby toadstool stem. Use the tip of the knife to carefully graze small round circles from the pink 'stool' part of the radish to expose the white flesh and make a polka-dot pattern. Set aside on a plate until you've crafted all of them. Magic.

RADISH ROSES

Grab a bunch o' radishes and trim the leaves and root from the top and bottom. Place one flat side on a board and, using a small sharp knife, cut slices down around the edge, keeping each piece still attached at the bottom. Then, work your knife inwards by a couple of millimetres to make another circle of petals. Continue to do this as far as you can inside each radish. Drop them into a bowl of iced water overnight and they'll open and flower. When ready to serve, place on a plate, with a couple of large flat-leaf parsley leaves positioned underneath. Really it's too, too exciting.

STRAWBERRY FROUFROU FANS

Take an unhulled strawberry and make several cuts lengthways with a small sharp knife from the stalk to the tip. Gently twist the strawberry to fan out the slices. Sweet.

SUGARED MINT LEAVES

Place the mint leaves on a board and make sure they're completely dry. Brush very lightly with beaten egg white, then dip them into granulated sugar. Place them on a wire rack and leave to dry out in a warm place. Voila.

STORAGE

All of the recipes in my book make a cornucopia of treats – there are enough for you to eat in secret before tea even gets underway. This is called 'quality control'. If there happens to be some left, you may serve them to your guests; if not, send out for a pizza. On the mere chance there may be anything left over when your guests have departed, and let us face facts chums, it is unlikely, here are a few notes on how you can keep them tasting as fresh and perky as *moi*.

CAKES

Store in an airtight container in a cool place. Don't chill or the lovely light sponge will turn into a loofa. Enjoy within two days if filled with fresh cream, or three days if filled with buttercream. I really can't believe I bothered to write that.

All the cakes freeze well, including the ones filled with buttercream. Just remember to pack them in an airtight container, so that nothing falls on top of them, like your mouth or a passing herd of hungry children, pie-curious dads, puppy dogs, lamas or indeed a passing elephant with a penchant for buttercream.

★ Open-freeze the **Marmalade Cake** (page 64) on a baking sheet first, then once the topping is firm, wrap well in clingfilm and freeze for up to one month. When you are ready to chow down, remove the clingfilm first (yes, I am required by law to remind you) then place in a cool place to thaw gradually and you are off.

★ The **Jaffa Madeleines** (page 52) should be frozen without their chocolate coating, then dipped before serving.

★ The **Top-notch Chocolate Truffle Cake** (page 70) is best frozen unsliced without the topping and truffles.

★ The **Malted Tea Loaves** (page 51) freeze perfectly and can be wrapped individually or together, depending on how grand your appliance.

MERINGUES

These will keep for up to a fortnight stored – unfilled – in an airtight container. They can't be frozen, though, so please don't chuck them in the freezer and then send me weepy emails. Once filled with fresh cream, eat them asap.

PROFITEROLES

Profiteroles should be stored in an airtight container – unfilled and unsliced – and will keep for up to three days. If you want to freeze them, wrap well in clingfilm and store in an airtight container, then thaw overnight.

SHORTBREAD AND BISCUITS

★ The **Petticoat Tails with Lavender and Honey** (page 62) and **Sea Salt Millionaire's Shortbread** (page 64) should be stored in an airtight tin and will keep for up to five days, otherwise they'll go Mr Floppy. You can freeze them, too. Swaddle them in clingfilm and freeze for up to a month.

★ The **Jammie Hearts** (page 59) will store well, unfilled, in an airtight container for up to five days. Once filled eat within a day.

★ The nutty biscuit bases of the **Hazelnut Tarts with Strawberries** (page 99) freeze awfully well. Just wrap the discettes well in clingfilm. Once out of the freezer, they will be ready to assemble in around half an hour.

PASTRY

★ The pastry of all the mini tarts (pages 85, 95 and 99) can be frozen for up to one month, either once it is made, or once the tin has been lined. Simply line the tin with pastry, wrap it in clingfilm and store in the freezer. These can be baked from frozen, too, but may take a few minutes longer depending on how long they've been stored in there.

★ The **millefeuille pastry bases** (page 100) can be made up to a week before and kept in an airtight container, dontcha know.

SCONES

★ **Scones** (page 44) are best made fresh and eaten warm from the oven, if you guzzle them all before Chantal and Pinotnoire arrive, it only takes 30 minutes to whip up another batch. But if you do want to make them ahead or have a few left over, wrap them in a bit of clingfilm and store in an airtight container for up to a day, or freeze for up to a month. Heat through on a baking sheet in a warm oven before serving.

★ The **Little Apple Strudels** (page 92), **Brandy Snaps** (page 91) and **Churros** (page 102) are all best made and enjoyed when fresh.

DRINKS

★ **Earl Grey Vodka** (page 120) needs a good couple of weeks to mature, so store in the fridge or a cold pantry during this time.

★ **Ginger Cordial with Mint and Lemon** (page 110) and **Sicilian Lemonade** (page 112) cordials both store brilliantly in the fridge and can be kept there for up to two weeks.

★ **Miss Hope and Mr Greenwood** can be wrapped in clingfilm and may toddle on for a few more years if stored at the seaside with a bottle of Hendrick's and a hammock.

PURVEYORS OF
HOPE
AND
GREENWOOD
SPLENDID GOODS ®

SPLENDID
SAVOURIES

CUCUMBER SANDWICHES WITH STRAWBERRIES AND MINT

★ **Makes 4 rounds**

★ **Take 15 minutes to make; plus 10 minutes to contemplate what a wonderful and weird concoction it is.**

4–6 fresh mint leaves, freshly chopped
4 tsp top-notch mayonnaise
Around a quarter of a jolly cucumber
4 medium strawberries
A little softened butter
8 slices white bread
Salt and freshly ground black pepper

EXPOSED: SEASHELL ATTACK
It was definitely my sister who dunnit. Defo. Not me, no, no.

This recipe comes courtesy of my mum, Granny Hope. Originally a plump strawberry, cool cucumber and tingly mint salad, I have now sandwiched the ingredients in white bread, not brown – this is important.

My mum made the salad for her neighbour Betty's wedding buffet. As the wedding music wafted over the cobbles, Granny Hope set out, proudly carrying her strawberry salad contribution. Alas, she was unceremoniously catapulted over an ill-placed giant seashell, splattered the salad up the coalhouse door and broke her leg in the bargain. How the seashell got there, I can't imagine. It remains a family mystery to this day.

★ Stir the mint, mayonnaise and a little seasoning together in a bowl. Put your finger in and have a lick; permission granted.
★ Peel the cucumber and slice it very finely. Hull the strawberries and finely slice them too.
★ Butter all the bread and lay the cucumbers and strawberries on top of the butter to cover four of the slices. Spread a little mint mayonnaise over the remaining four slices of buttered bread.
★ Sandwich the two halves together, then cut the crusts off in a lady-like way. Cut into quarter triangles and eat washed down with a glass of fizzy.

SALT BEEF WITH MUSTARD MAYO AND GHERKINS ON RYE

Salt beef should not be mistaken for corned beef or 'bully beef'. It is beef brisket, which has been dry cured or pickled in brine. Buy it from good delis or St Waitrose. I have teamed it with hot mustard mayonnaise, gherkins and rye bread. It was Doctor J C Browne who invented salt beef as a cure for rheumatism, gout and hiccups, colds, coughs and bronchitis, spasms, hysteria, palpitations and loneliness. Loser.

★ Preheat the oven to 200°C/400°F/Gas 6. Butter the bread, then trim the crusts off and cut each slice in half, to make two rectangles. Push the bread buttered-side down into the holes of the mince pie tin and squish it down a bit to squash it into the shape of the tin. Bake in the oven for 8–10 minutes until golden and crisp. Top stuff.
★ Remove the bread from the tin and leave to cool. Introduce the mayonnaise to the mustard in a bowl, stir them together and divide the mayo equally among the bread nests. Slice each piece of salt beef in half, wrap each one into a tight roll and place it on top of the mayo mixture.
★ Add a cherry tomato wedge and gherkin slice on the top of each filled nest, finishing with a trembling parsley leaf garnish.

★ **Makes 12 boats**

★ **Take 25 minutes to make and 5 minutes to get the lid off the gherkins.**

A little softened butter
6 thin slices light rye bread
1½ tbsp mayonnaise
1½ tsp grainy mustard
6 thin slices salt beef
2 cherry tomatoes, each cut into six wedges
6 cocktail gherkins, halved lengthways
12 leaves of flat-leaf parsley, to garnish

Traditional smooth-sided mince pie tin

ASPARAGUS AND PROSCIUTTO LILIES

★ **Makes 8 celebratory horns**

★ **Take 20 minutes to make.**

8 thin asparagus
  tips, cut to 6cm
  (2½in) lengths
4 small slices
  white bread
4 small slices
  brown bread
A little softened
  butter
3–4 slices
  prosciutto
75g (3oz) cream
  cheese
  (or Primula
  cheese spread,
  the toothpaste
  of cheeses)

Piping bag
  (optional)

In honour of Miss Lily Lovelace's 21st birthday, 2 Eton Square, London WC1, I bring you an afternoon treat: a dainty little cream cheese cone with a stamen of asparagus and a sliver of prosciutto. Miss Lily has asked me to relay the following statement to her family and friends:

'Yo' w'assup, iz ma birfday, iz ma birfday, I'm gonna pardee, I'm gonna pardee, safe, is it?'

★ Bring a small pan of water to the boil and add the asparagus. Cook for 2–3 minutes until just tender. Drain and cool quickly under cold running water. Safe.

★ Cut the crusts off each slice of bread, to make squares measuring 6 x 6cm (2½ x 2½in). This may look wasteful but it's important to get the right size square to make a dainty horn. Use a knife to round one corner of each slice. Spread each with butter. Sweet.

★ Cover the buttered side of each bread slice with a little prosciutto, leaving a little gap on one side. Roll up the bread slices to make cone shapes, sticking them down along the buttered gap to secure them. Put the cream cheese into a piping bag fitted with a 6mm nozzle and squeeze a dollop into each horn, or use a teaspoon to delicately fill them. If you're using Primula cheese spread, just squeeze it directly into each horn from the tube. Stick an asparagus tip into each horn and serve, with a jug of euphemisms on the side.

GOLDEN SALMON SANDWICHES WITH MINT JELLY

★ **Serves 1; double up if the mist lifts and your mates can get over to your castle.**

★ **Takes 10 minutes to make; plus 5 minutes to toss a caber.**

A little softened butter
2 slices brown bread
1 tbsp mint jelly
2 small slices smoked salmon
A little vegetable oil

A deep mist muffles down low over the purple heather-rolled hills of Scotland. Virginia McKenna is starving and cannot get to the shops – bad luck lassie. Deftly, she throws together a sandwich of smoked salmon and mint jelly, which she fries in butter. An unlikely combination, you may think. But wait…

'Aye, it's a wee winner!' she cries. Catching up her cloak and tam, she sets out, uncaring of the treacherous weather, to Gordon Jackson's castle for a celebratory dram of Irn Bru.

★ Butter the slices of bread on the outside. Yes, the outside. Spread the inside of one slice with the mint jelly, and rest the smoked salmon slices on top. Sandwich the two bits of bread into a sandwich, obviously.
★ Heat a frying pan over a medium heat until rather hot, then add a splooshette of the oil. Slide the buttered-on-the-outside sandwich into the pan and cook for 2–3 minutes until the bottom of the sandwich is delightfully golden. Fling it over and fry until golden on the other side. Slice and serve to Gordon Jackson, if he's about.

LOW CALORIE OPTION FROM YOURS TRULY

Butter the slices of bread on the inside. Spread one half with the mint jelly and wedge a couple of smoked salmon slices on top. Cover with peeled, finely sliced cucumber, season with freshly ground black pepper and put the other buttered slice of bread on top. Cut off the crusts, feed the salmon from these bits to the cat and cut the sandwich into probing fingers (see photo on the cover).

FIG AND PECORINO CRESCIA WITH HONEY

★ **Makes 16 crescia**

★ **Take 30 minutes to make; plus 1 hour 30 minutes chilling, and 30 minutes to calm Mr Greenwood down.**

100g (3½oz) plain flour
1 medium egg, beaten
15g (½oz) lard, at room
   temperature. Yes, lard.
   This is very important.

For the topping
Thick-set honey, for
   spreading
A young pecorino, for
   shaving
2 ripe figs
A handful of rocket leaves
Freshly ground black
   pepper

Many summers ago, when Mr Greenwood had snake hips, he took a sun-kissed holiday to the Le Marche region in Italy. It was here in a small hill-proud town, red roofed and dust cobbled, that he first laid eyes on Patricia; the cling of her gypsy top, the sway of her hips and her amazing little crescia flat breads – mounted by fresh figs over which she poured local honey and scattered shavings of young pecorino. In stumbling, stilted Italian, Mr Greenwood declared his undying love for Patricia and her perfectly formed crescia. In return, she shared her secret recipe.

★ Sift the flour into a medium bowl and add the egg. Stir together with a knife, to make a roughboy dough. Stick your hands in there and work the mixture together, mopping up any dry bits of flour, until it feels smooth and elastic – it's the same technique as when you're making bread. Wrap in clingfilm and chill for 30 minutes.
★ Put the lard in a cup and squish down with a spoon to soften (sorry). Work it until it looks like a paste.
★ Lightly dust a clean board with flour and roll out the chilled dough into a large rectangle measuring around 20 x 24cm (8 x 9½in). Spread the softened lard all over it in a thin layer, then roll it up tightly from the longest edge. Cut the dough across its length into 16 even-sized pieces, put on a plate and chill for up to one hour until firm.
★ Dust a clean board generously with flour and roll out each

P.T.O.

OTHER SECRETS
Reluctantly, Patricia shared with Mr G her other secret: she was indeed a bloke.

piece of chilled dough to make a circle measuring around 7cm (2¾in) in diameter. Heat a heavy-based frying pan on the hob until hot and cook the dough circles in batches for a couple of minutes on each side. They are ready to turn when the tops turn a golden yellow and the undersides are sun-kissed golden.

★ Spread a little honey on each crescia and top with some pecorino shavings. Slice each fig into thin wedges, then put three slivers of fig on top of each crescia with some more pecorino shavings, a few leaves of rocket and a sprinkling of black pepper.

CURRIED EGG BRIDGE ROLLS WITH PEA SHOOTS

Violet, James and Enid are admiring the fishpond. Grandpapa has been busy training his prize-winning koi carp all day. 'It's time for tea, Grandpapa!' shouts Violet for the fifth time. 'Cook's whipped up some delish little bridge rolls with your favourite curried egg, a smidge of mango chutters and some jolly good pea shoots. You can't stay down there forever, your fingers will go all pruney.'

★ Please sift the flours into a bowl, adding any granary bits left in the sieve into the bowl. Thank you. Stir in the yeast and salt. Add 125–150ml (4–5fl oz) lukewarm water and stir in with a knife until well combined.

★ Tip the craggy dough out onto a board and knead well for 5–10 minutes to make a soft dough. Add a little more water if you think it needs it, but resist adding any more flour when kneading – it should be slightly sticky. Put the dough back in the bowl, cover with a saucepan lid and set aside in a warm place (in a sunny spot, or near a radiator) for 40 minutes to rise until doubled in size. Hurrah!

★ Scrape the dough out of the bowl onto a board and divide it into 10 equal-sized pieces. Roll each into a little saucisson shape around 5cm (2in) long, and put on a well-floured baking sheet. Dispatch the dough to a warm place to prove for 30 minutes. Preheat the oven to 200°C/400°F/Gas 6.

P.T.O.

★ **Makes 10 rolls, or 20 polite open sandwiches**

★ **Take 1 hour to make; plus proving and rising time, and 5 minutes for Grandpapa to swim through the castle.**

For the rolls
100g (4oz) plain white flour, plus 1 tbsp to dust
100g (4oz) strong granary bread flour
½ tsp dried yeast
¼ tsp salt

For the curried egg mayonnaise
6 medium eggs, at room temperature
4–6 heaped tsp mayonnaise
1 tsp mild curry powder
1 tbsp mango chutney, plus extra for drizzling
Salt and freshly ground black pepper
Pea shoots, to garnish

★ Bake the bread in the oven for around 15 minutes until the rolls sound hollow when tapped on the underside. Remove from the baking sheet and leave to cool on a wire rack.

★ Put the eggs in a pan of cold water over a low to medium heat, cover with a lid and bring them to a simmer. Boil for 7 minutes. Lift them out carefully and plunge them into a bowl of cold water, like Ethel Merman, then peel. Mash the eggs in a bowl with a fork, adding the mayonnaise, curry powder, mango chutney and a little seasoning. Cut each bridge roll in half horizontally and spoon a little curried egg mayonnaise on one half. Garnish with a pea shoot and a little extra mango chutney, then serve.

WHITBY KIPPER
PATE SANDWICHES

The grey sea smacks, spitting into the bay, gulls wheel overhead, sirens screeching. The Priory watches with blind arches the fishermen of Whitby hunt for tiger-skinned mackerel. Captain Joe is playing cards, but his concentration is as thin as his breath. On the wet quay Count Dracula, Prince of Darkness, steps silently ashore, pressed darkly into the corner shadows. Soon it will be dusk and he will be stalking his prey, his soul eternally hungry.

'Oi! Fang-Face!' yells Captain Joe, 'have you eaten my Kipper Pâté sandwiches again?'

★ Pin-bone the kipper (or mackerel) to remove any lickle bones. Skin the fish, then break up the flesh and put it in a blender or small food processor with the mayonnaise and lemon juice. Season and blitz to make a lovely smooth pâté. You may need to push the mixture back down into the bowl of the blender every now and then to make sure all the fish is blended.

★ Scrape the pâté into a bowl and stir in the chopped dill.

★ Cut one shape from each slice of bread using the sandwich cutters. Butter one side of four white shapes, and four brown. Spread the pâté over the unbuttered bread shapes, then top with the buttered slices, to make eight sandwiches, half white, half brown bread. To serve, arrange on a platter and garnish with cucumber twists (see page 12), lemon wedges and dill sprigs.

★ **Makes 8 sandwiches**

★ **Take 20 minutes to make, and about 8 hours for a night of the living dead.**

75g (3oz) cooked smoked kipper or smoked mackerel
1–2 tbsp mayonnaise
Juice of ½ lemon, plus 1 lemon cut into wedges, to garnish
1 tbsp freshly chopped dill, plus extra to garnish
8 small slices white bread
8 small slices brown bread
A little softened butter
Cucumber Twists (see page 12), to garnish
Salt and freshly ground black pepper

Sandwich cutters; such as Tala card pattern cutters (please see the end of this book for stockists)

POTTED PRAWNS WITH DILL AND MELBA TOAST

★ **Makes 12 micro eggcups or four 150ml ramekins**

★ **Takes 20 hearty minutes to make; plus chilling on deck.**

300g (11oz) cooked, peeled prawns
A couple of pinches of cayenne pepper
1 tbsp freshly chopped dill, plus extra to garnish
250g pack unsalted butter
1 lemon slice, cut into wedgettes
6 slices granary bread
Salt and freshly ground black pepper

12 eggcups or four 150ml ramekins

Handy Tip
Always check for barnacles below the water line.

Flecked with dill and sealed with a kiss of clarified butter, these potted prawns were Cap'n Broderick Leadfoot's preferred snack. The pirate Captain, attired – as was his penchant – entirely in Marie-rose tulle, often dined on board his ship, the *Thunder of Atlantis*, with his soulmate Nigel, who was a dab hand at Melba toast, eye-patch sequin application and naked squid wrestling.

★ Mix the prawns, cayenne and dill in a bowl, and season liberally. Divide the pinky-perky mixture among 12 egg cups or four ramekins.
★ Splat the butter in a small pan and heat gently to melt. When it has been sufficiently tortured and has started to simmer, it will have separated into a foamy skin and clear yellow liquid underneath. Scoop off the frothy top (not to be misconstrued) with a spoon and bin it.
★ Pour the clarified butter equally over each of the prawny pots. Delight with a sprig of dill and lemon wedgette on top of each pot, and chill for 2–3 hours until set. (If you want to store these for longer, they will keep well, covered with clingfilm, in the fridge for up to three days.)
★ Preheat the grill and toast the bread. Cut the crusts off, then cut each slice horizontally between the toasted crusts using a sharp knife or cutlass so it is as thin as a pirate captain's negligee. Slice into triangles and toast the untoasted side until golden and curlified. Serve with the chilled potted prawns.

SAUSAGE, SAGE AND APPLE ROLLS

Long ago there was a land called Koombaland (meaning 'coiled rope'), where fish jumped brightly in the tarns and sheep stood gathered in the heather. It was here that the local butcher, Scragend Bob, invented the sausage roll; here made with tart apples, sage and the local speciality sausage, coiled like a rope, and filled with chunks of pork. Over centuries we have come to know this as the Koombaland – or Cumberland – sausage.

★ Preheat the oven to 200°C/400°F/Gas 6. Run a sharp knife down the length of each sausage to split the skins, and slip the meat out and into a bowl. Add the apple and sage, mix well and put to one side.
★ Cut the pastry in half. Roll out one piece on a lightly floured clean work surface until it measures around 30 x 20cm (12 x 8in).
★ Divide the sausage meat into four lumps in the bowl. Take one lump, sprinkle flour over your hands and roll the lump into a long sausage-dog shape to fit the length of the rolled pastry. Place the sausage meat near one long edge. Do the same with a second lump, shaping it and placing it near the other long edge. Cut through the pastry down the middle to separate the two rolls. Brush the egg over each length, then roll up to enclose the sausage meat, with the seam underneath. Trim the ends, then carefully cut at 3cm (1¼in) intervals to make about 17 splendid little rolls. Brush each with the beaten egg, stick a sage leaf on top and brush with another slick of egg. Put all the rolls on a large baking sheet.
★ Repeat the method above to make the remaining 17 rolls. Bake in the oven for 25 minutes until they are golden all over. Serve warm.

★ **Makes around 34 rolls**

★ **Take 55 minutes to make, and 30 minutes to get over the Koombaland joke.**

450g (1lb) Cumberland sausages
75g (3oz) peeled and cored tart cooking apple (such as Bramley), grated
4 large sage leaves, chopped, plus 36 small leaves to garnish
500g pack shortcrust pastry
A little plain flour, to dust
1 medium egg, beaten

ENGLISH MINI MUFFINS WITH 'M' AND 'X'

★ **Makes 24 mufties**

★ **Take 40 minutes to make and overnight to crease your trousers.**

40g (1½oz) salted butter, melted and cooled, plus extra for greasing
225g (8oz) self-raising flour
½ tsp salt
½ tsp ground white pepper
100g (4oz) finely chopped ham
20g (¾oz) Cheddar, finely grated
1 tsp English mustard powder
1 tbsp freshly chopped parsley
150ml (5fl oz) natural yogurt
1 large egg
100ml (4fl oz) milk

For the filling
60g (2½oz) softened salted butter
A couple of dashes of cayenne pepper
A box of cress

24-hole mini-muffin tin
Piping bag and star nozzle

Johnny 'Boffer' Jenkins is a well turned out gentleman. He knows to acknowledge a lady on a tram with a lift of his trilby. He also knows a good egg muffin when he spies one, especially one made with ham, British Cheddar and English mustard. Anything else would just not be cricket.

★ Preheat the oven to 200°C/400°F/Gas 6. Grease the mini-muffin tin generously with butter.

★ Sift the flour into a medium bowl. Add the salt and pepper, ham, cheese, mustard powder and parsley. Toss everything together. Steady on, old man; watch the mustard on the waistcoat.

★ Mix the cooled, melted butter, yogurt, egg and milk together in a bowl. Beat the blighter. Make a well in the middle of the flour mixture and pour in the wet mixture. Use firm, fast strokes with a large metal spoon to bring the two mixtures together – don't worry if there are
a few floury patches, matron will clean them up.

★ Spoon the mixture equally among the greased tin holes and bake in the oven for 15–20 minutes. Leave to cool for a minute or two, then use a spatula to gently prise them out of the tin, and leave to cool completely on a wire rack.

★ Beat together the butter and cayenne pepper.

★ Slice the top off each mini muffin and set the tops aside. Pipe a rose of cayenne butter on top of each muffin, or spread the butter on with a knife, then top the butter with cress and replace the muffin hat – gentlemen should always wear hats. Serve immediately.

QUAIL SCOTCH EGGS WITH CHIN'S CHILLI SAUCE

★ **Makes 12 phenomenal Scotch eggs, and around 700g (24oz) of chutney**

★ **Take around 2 hours to make.**

12 quails' eggs
2 generous tbsp plain flour
2 medium hen's eggs,
  beaten
50g (2oz) dried
  breadcrumbs
8 Lincolnshire sausages
Around 2 litres (70fl oz)
  vegetable oil, for deep-
  frying
Salt and freshly ground
  black pepper

For Chin's chilli sauce
1 small fresh pineapple
2 large red chillies, stalk
  removed
1 tsp chilli flakes
6 garlic cloves, peeled
2 large tomatoes
500ml (17fl oz) white
  wine vinegar
200g (7oz) golden caster
  sugar
1 tsp salt

Meet Chin. Chin is from Kuala Lumpur (which is somewhere you go to get dengue fever). I have been stealing Chin's chilli sauce from the Sugar HQ fridge for some years now, adding it to my soup, pasta and cheese on toast, but after a heated exchange in a foreign tongue (I have no idea what she said) I managed to prize the recipe out of her so you can all have a lash. It is hot with chillies, sour with vinegar and sweet with pineapple. With peppery Lincolnshire sausage and quails' eggs, it is absolutely phenomenal.

★ To make the chilli sauce, top, tail and peel the pineapple and remove any remaining black 'eyes'. Cut into quarters lengthways, and slice the core from each segment. Chop each segment into rough chunks and blitz in a food processor with the chillies, garlic cloves and tomatoes to make a luscious sauce.

★ Tip the sauce into a large stainless steel pan and add the vinegar, sugar, chilli flakes and salt. Stir, and bring it to the boil. Simmer the sauce, uncovered, over a low heat, for 1 hour until thick, stirring from time to time. Just before the hour's up, sterilise two jars: wash them, and their lids, in hot water, then fill with boiling water and pour the water back out immediately. Pot the hot sauce into the sterilised jars, cover with the lids and keep in a cool place. Unopened, the sauce will keep well in the fridge for up to three months. Once opened, store it in the fridge for up to two weeks.

★ For the Scotch eggs, boil some water in a pan and cook the quails' eggs over a medium heat for 3 minutes, then transfer them to a bowl of cold water to cool. Once cool, very carefully peel the shells off the eggs and put them on a plate.

★ Put the flour in a shallow bowl and season well. Put the eggs in another shallow bowl and put the breadcrumbs in a third shallow bowl. Focus, please.

★ Use a knife to score and split the skin along the length of each sausage. Scoop out the sausage meat and put it in a clean bowl, keeping the sausage shape as much as possible. Take two-thirds of each sausage and gently flatten – wet your hands to prevent the sausage meat sticking to them. Wrap the sausage meat around a quail egg, making sure the egg is completely covered. Repeat until you've done all the eggs.

★ Now roll each sausage-egg ball in the seasoned flour, then in the egg and then in the breadcrumbs. Put your balls on a plate. Your hands will be pretty sticky by the end but keep going until you've covered all the eggs.

★ Heat the oil in a large deep pan over a medium heat until a cube of fresh bread cooks and turns golden in around 30 seconds. Carefully drop the eggs into the hot oil in batches, three at a time – plop, plop, plop – and sizzle for 6–7 minutes until dark golden. Remove from the sizzling oil with a slotted spoon, and drain on kitchen paper. Cut one open to check the sausage meat is cooked all the way through. If it's not cooked through, return the eggs to oil to cook for another minute or two. Serve immediately, while they are still warm, with Chin's amazing chilli sauce.

Chin says:
'Miss Hope, ini resipi rahsia aku, abang adik aku akan kerjakan kau kalau awak bongkarkan resipi ni!'

Aw bless, isn't she lovely?

WILD MUSHROOM VOL-AU-VENTS

★ **Makes 12 vols**

★ **Take 30 minutes to make, including baking and doing swan glides around the kitchen.**

12 frozen vol-au-vent cases (big cheat)
1 medium egg, beaten

For the mushroom filling
A knob of butter
A drizzle of vegetable oil
1 shallot, peeled and finely chopped
200g (7oz) wild mushrooms, cleaned and roughly chopped
2 tbsp crème fraîche
2 tsp Dijon mustard
The leaves pulled from 2 sprigs of thyme, plus extra sprigs to garnish
A drizzle of truffle oil (optional)
Salt and freshly ground black pepper

If you are ever in Cookham in July, you may be lucky enough to witness the quaint custom of swan upping, where the Queen of England takes to her rowing skiff in search of cygnets. She counts and weighs them and gives them a little tickle. In olden days she would have made then into a nice pie with a bit of mash potato and swan gravy. Now she settles for a puff pastry case filled with wild mushrooms in a creamy mustard sauce, with a drizzle of truffle oil.

★ Preheat the oven to 220°C/425°F/Gas 7. Put the vol-au-vent cases on a baking sheet and brush the outside edge of each case with the beaten egg. Bake in the oven for 13–15 minutes until puffed up and golden like a queen's ball gown.
★ Heat the butter and oil in a pan. When the butter has melted and the foaming died down, add the chopped shallot and cook over a gentle heat for 2–3 minutes until softened. Add the mushrooms and continue to cook for 2–3 minutes until golden. Stir in the crème fraîche, mustard and thyme leaves and cook for 1 more minute, seasoning well.
★ Spoon the mushroom mixture into the vol-au-vent cases, drizzling each with a touch of truffle oil (if using), and garnish with a sprig of thyme and serve.

THE KING OF ENGLAND
Sometimes the King of England goes along for the ride; his webbed feet are well suited for swimming.

CRAB AND SAMPHIRE TARTS

A top-notch little tart filled with white and dark crab meat, a lemon and a Tabasco zing. Mr G and I tramp welly-clad to greet the young samphire plant as it pokes its seaweed-green fingers through the big blue-skied, mud-rich north Norfolk coast. Abundant in the summer months, it nestles in sea-salt inlets between Thornham and the Burnhams, or the slippery creeks around Morston, Cley and Waitrose.

★ Preheat the oven to 190°C/375°F/Gas 5.

★ Unroll out the pastry on a lightly floured board. Cut out 20 rounds using a 6cm (2½in) round cutter and use 12 rounds to line the holes of the mince pie tin. Prick the base of each a couple of times with a fork and shove in the oven for 12–15 minutes until golden. Remove from the tin and place on a wire rack to cool. Repeat with the remaining eight pastry rounds. Turn off the oven, twit.

★ Toss the vibrant green samphire into a pan of boiling water and cook for 1–2 minutes. Drain it well and tip it into a bowl with a generous knob of butter, a bit of S and P and a little freshly grated nutmeg.

★ Mix the brown crab meat in a bowl with the mayonnaise, add a tot of Tabasco and a bit more S and P. In a separate bowl, mix the white crab meat with the lemon zest and a squeeze of juice. Divide the brown crab meat mixture evenly among the 20 pastry cases. Top with the white crab meat and a sweet sprig of samphire. Grate over some more nutmeg and hide in the coat cupboard under the stairs until everyone has gone home/you have scoffed the lot.

★ **Makes 20 tarts**

★ **Take 50 minutes to make.**

375g chilled ready-rolled shortcrust pastry
A little plain flour, to dust
A small handful of samphire
A knob of butter
Whole nutmeg, for grating
100g (4oz) brown crab meat (Cromer, if you can)
2 tsp mayonnaise
Tabasco
100g (4oz) white crab meat
Zest and juice of ½ lemon
Salt and freshly ground black pepper

Traditional smooth-sided mince pie tin

FACT FROM THE NORFOLK TOURIST BOARD
For any of you not acquainted with Norfolk, it is a very nice place, despite the fact it has been taken over by enormous, intelligent mutated crabs. Fact.

PURVEYORS OF
HOPE
AND
GREENWOOD
SPLENDID GOODS ®

CREAMY CAKES,
BEAUTIFUL
BISCUITS AND
BRILLIANT
BREADS

BUTTERMILK SCONES WITH RASPBERRY JAM

★ **Makes 6 scone platform wedges**

★ **Take 35 minutes to make.**

225g (8oz) plain flour, sifted, plus extra to dust
50g (2oz) unsalted butter
1 tsp baking powder
25g (1oz) golden caster sugar
125ml (4½fl oz) buttermilk
Splash of milk (if needed)
Clotted cream and good raspberry jam, to serve
A punnet of raspberries, to serve

Please let me introduce you to the buttermilk scone, a homely, dutiful scone, bountiful with the promise of warm kitchens, sleepy cats and Aga Sagas. Wave hubby on his way, whistling cheerfully officewards, don a starched apron and get down to some good old-fashioned housewifery. Once you have made a buttermilk scone there will be no return to the bland scone of yesterday, no siree Bob. Speaking of things of the past, here is a picture of Jean next door in her crochet playsuit and mocha, suedette boots, taken yesterday.

★ Preheat the oven to 220°C/425°F/Gas 7. Line a baking sheet with baking parchment.
★ Dash the flour and butter into a bowl and rub the butter into the flour using your delicate girl hands, until the mixture looks like breadcrumbs. Stir in the baking powder, sugar and buttermilk with a wooden spoon to make a tip-top dough. Add a splash of milk if the mixture seems a tad dry. Tip the mixture out onto a lightly floured board and knead very gently to bring together into one harmonious lump.
★ Primp the dough into a round shape and use a knife to mark it into six wedges, clock-like, cutting down into the dough enough to mark them but not all the way through. Pop the promising round dough lump on the prepared baking sheet and place in the oven for 15–20 minutes until golden and glorious. Cool on a wire rack and serve with clotted cream, jam and raspberries.

Tip of the day, at no extra charge

To make small scones, pat or roll the dough until it's 2½cm (1in) thick. Use a 5cm (2in) round cutter to stamp out the rounds – you may need to re-roll once or twice, and you'll make 10 small scones, plus a piggly-wiggly runt (the little bit of dough at the end which is too small to be stamped out into a round). Bake in the oven for 12–15 minutes.

PASSION FRUIT FAIRY CAKES

Can I tell you that this is the cutest little fairy cake that ever sat on a plate? Can I tell you I am in love with this sponge-soft fluffy morsel, or that the splash of passion fruit purée dribbling down the chin of orange icing is the nearest thing to having a bubble bath with Colin Filth? Can I?

★ Cut the passion fruit for the cakes in half and scoop the seeds and the carnal fleshy bits into a sieve hanging manfully over a bowl. Use a wooden spoon to stir these bits furiously to extract the juice. Throw away the seeds (or compost them if you are a nice person and have a compost bin).

★ Preheat the oven to 180°C/350°F/Gas 4. Line the mini-muffin tin with paper cases. Put the butter and sugar in a bowl and beat with a wooden spoon or electric hand whisk until pale, soft and creamy, then gradually beat in the egg. Gently fold in the flour and add the vanilla extract and passion fruit juice. Mix until everything is beautifully combined. If the mixture seems very stiff, fold in a splash of milk, so that the mix drops off the spoon with ease.

★ Plop teaspoonfuls of the mixture into each paper case and bake in the oven for 15 minutes until golden. Take them out of the tin and cool on a wire rack.

★ Now for the icing. Beat the butter in a bowl and gradually add the icing sugar, beating the mixture until it is soft and dreamy. A splash of milk will help it on its way. It should be fairly stiff when you finish mixing (resisting temptation). Spoon the icing into a piping bag,

P.T.O.

★ **Makes 24 chin-dribblin' cakes**

★ **Take 45 minutes to make, and about 4 hours to make a life-size waterproof Colin Filth doll.**

Juice of 1 large, ripe
   passion fruit
110g (4¼oz) softened
   unsalted butter
110g (4¼oz) golden
   caster sugar
1 large egg, beaten
110g (4¼oz) self-raising
   flour, sifted
1 tsp vanilla extract
Splash of milk (if needed)

For the icing and decoration
100g (4oz) softened
   unsalted butter
300g (11oz) icing sugar,
   plus extra to dust
Splash of milk
6 ripe passion fruit

One 24-hole mini-muffin
   tin
24 mini-muffin paper
   cases
Piping bag

fitted with a 1cm (½in) star nozzle, and pipe a delightful perky swirl on top of each cooled cake. Go as high as you can.

★ Halve the passion fruit for the decoration and scoop the seeds and juice into a sieve plonked over a small pan. Stir like a demon again to extract the juice, and save the seeds. Heat the juice for about 1 minute until it is thick, syrupy and sticky. Scrape it into a bowl and add a spoonful of the seeds. Spoon a drizzle of the juice and seeds over each cake and call Colin; he's been on that computer for ages. Men.

Dear Colin Filth
Please dribble on me.

SINGING HINNIES

Deep in the Geordie winter Wor Mam is rustling up some delicious little drop scones on a hot griddle. As they cook, they sizzle or 'sing'. For those of you in the namby-pamby south, 'hinnie' is a term of endearment meaning 'honey'. For example:

Cherie Coal: 'Are the scones ready fre us's teas, Wor Mam? Ant and Dec will be heor in a minute.'

Wor Mam: 'Not yet, they are still singing, hinnie. Hev a pint of The Toon Broon Ale while ah put some fishies on a little dishy, bonnie lass.'

★ Sift the flour, cream of tartar and bicarbonate of soda into a bowl. Rub in the butter and lard – yes, lard – this give the hinnie its characteristic flakiness.

★ Stir in the currants and add 1 tablespoon of milk. Mix with the blade of a knife to make a soft dough, adding another tablespoon of milk if needed. Knead lightly then roll out on a lightly floured board to a thickness of 0.5cm (¼in) and cut out 3.5cm (1¼in) rounds using a round cutter.

★ Heat a heavy-based griddle pan and add a little lard. Once melted, fry the hinnies on each side until cooked through and a rich golden brown. If you want to keep the whole batch warm, put them on a baking sheet in the oven, heated to around 100°C/200°F/Gas ½.

★ Serve with a slick of butter and a soupçon of plum jam. Should there be any left over, which is doubtful, store them in a sealable container for up to two days, or freeze for up to one month.

★ **Makes around 46 mini hinnies**

★ **Take 30 minutes to make, and 10 minutes to pop on a black and white frock.**

200g (7oz) plain flour, plus extra to dust
⅛ tsp cream of tartar
¼ tsp bicarbonate of soda
50g (2oz) unsalted butter
50g (2oz) lard, plus extra for frying
75g (3oz) currants
1–2 tbsp milk
Butter and plum jam, to serve

SOME OTHER GEORDIE PHRASES
'Ah wes palatick' = 'I had such a smashing time, thank you ever so.'
'Howay doon to the big market fer a pint of Dog, bonnie lass?' = 'Would you care to join me in a glass of bubbly in a high class establishment, darling?'
'Mindshesweelstacked' = 'Golly gosh, are they real?'

MALTED TEA LOAVES

Terry is hanging out the washing. It's a blustery day in Barnet – in fact it's been a blustery week; a good week for washing. She is a neighbourly sort, chatting happily over the fence, passing the time of day.

'Time,' says Terry, 'for a nice cuppa and some malted tea loaf.'

Terry loves malted tea loaf. She loves the mixed spice, the plump raisins, the black treacle and the malty goodness. Terry's husband is buried under the crazy paving, but she likes to keep his shirts clean. She is good wife, a serial killer, but a good wife.

★ Put the yeast in a small bowl and pour in a good splash of milk. Give it a stir, and set aside for a few minutes to dissolve the yeast.

★ Put the remaining ingredients into a large bowl. Make a well in the centre and add the yeasted mixture and the remaining milk and stir everything together with a spoon or a round-bladed knife to make a craggy dough. Knead the dough on a lightly floured board for 5–10 minutes until soft and sticky. Plonk it back in the bowl, cover with a saucepan lid, and leave to rise for 45 minutes.

★ Tip the dough onto a lightly floured board and knead gently. Divide the dough into nine even-sized pieces. Shape each one and use to fill the cake mould holes. Set aside in a warm place (somewhere a cat might like) to prove for 30 minutes. Preheat the oven to 200°C/400°F/Gas 6.

★ Bake in the oven for 20 minutes until risen and golden. Remove the mini loaves from the tin and serve with butter while they're still warm.

★ **Makes 9 mini loaves**

★ **Take 40 minutes to make; plus rising and proving time. And a split second to hit your husband with a toaster.**

1 tsp dried yeast
175ml (6fl oz) warm milk
300g (11oz) plain flour,
    plus extra to dust
1 tsp mixed spice
75g (3oz) raisins
1 tbsp black treacle
    or molasses sugar
40g (1½oz) malt extract
25g (1oz) butter, plus
    extra for serving
½ tsp salt

9-hole cake mould (please
    see the end of this book
    for stockists)

JAFFA MADELEINES

★ **Makes 12 love-at-first-bite seashells**

★ **Take 45 minutes to make; plus cooling, and 20 minutes to twirl your Proust moustache.**

75g (3oz) unsalted butter, melted and cooled, plus extra for greasing
75g (3oz) self-raising flour, plus extra to dust
75g (3oz) golden caster sugar
1 extra large egg
Zest of 1 orange
Around 200g (7oz) good quality milk chocolate, to decorate

12-hole Madeleine tin
Chocolate thermometer (optional)

I was amoured of this delicious, seashell-shaped sponge cake as soon as I spied it in The Steak Bake Emporium. I hastily finished my Breakfast For Less and tucked into this dainty Madeleine, dipped as it was in a little milk chocolate and infused with orange zest. I raised it to my lips, too eagerly perhaps… a shudder ran through my body, it was a big shudder. It reminded me of my dear, dear chum, the humble Jaffa Cake, though considerably more refined. All at once, our drab grey house became a thing of beauty, French doors beckoning me to a little Juliette balcony overlooking the Mr Big Burger car park.

★ Preheat the oven to 180°C/350°F/Gas 4. Grease the holes of the Madeleine tin with butter, then dust each hole generously with flour, tipping away any excess.

★ Place the sugar and egg in a bowl and whisk for about 5 minutes until the mixture is thick and beautifully moussey, and the whisk – lifted out of the bowl – leaves ribbon trails of mixture that just hold their shape.

★ Sift the flour into the bowl, and add the orange zest and melted butter. Fold everything together with a large metal spoon, using short firm strokes, to make sure all the flour has been incorporated. Divide the mixture among the holes and bake in the oven for 10–15 minutes until adorably golden brown. Turn the tray around halfway through cooking to make sure the Madeleines cook evenly. Lift them out of the tin and leave to cool on a wire rack.

★ Once cool, prepare the milk chocolate. If you are going to temper the chocolate so it has a lovely brittle snap and doesn't cloud on cooling, you'll need a chocolate thermometer. Heat 5cm (2in) water in a pan. Pop the chocolate a heatproof bowl on top of the pan, making sure the bottom of the bowl is not touching the water. Melt the chocolate gently. Once melted, put the thermometer into the chocolate and wait until it drops to 30–31°C (86–88°F). As soon as it reaches this temperature, shove a Madeleine into the chocolate and set aside to cool on baking parchment. If you can't be bothered with the tempering business just melt the chocolate, pour it into a little bowl and ask your guests to dunk.

*Marcel Greenwood (1871–1922) 'Memories of the Old Kent Road'

PISTACHIO KISSES

★ **Makes 30 streetwise meringues**

★ **Take 1 hour 30 minutes to make; plus chillaxin' time.**

40g (1½oz) shelled
  pistachios
100g (3½oz) golden
  caster sugar
2 medium egg whites
50g (2oz) dark chocolate,
  broken into pieces

Piping bag

Squirrel Greenwood, our favourite tough-nut, and Snoop Bunny, his bezzie, are shopping for nuts in Croydon. He is spoilt for choice; hazelnuts, walnuts, pistachios and a Happy Bus of window lickers. Squirrel Greenwood settles for a bag o' pistachios because his mummy is making Pistachio Kisses filled with chocolate for tea and he loves his mummy.

'Word,' says SQ to SB. 'See ya on the flip-side and ting. Fo'shizzle.'

★ Preheat the oven to 130°C/250°F/Gas ½. Line two baking sheets with baking parchment. Isit.

★ Put the pistachios in a food processor with 1 teaspoon of the sugar and whiz until finely chopped.

★ Pop the egg whites in a spotlessly clean grease-free bowl. Whisk with an electric hand whisk until soft peaks form. Add the rest of the sugar, a spoonful at a time, whisking well between each addition, and continuing to whisk until stiff, smooth and glossy, yo' feel me?

★ Use a large metal spoon to gently fold the chopped pistachios into the meringue mix. Spoon the mixture into a piping bag, fitted with a 1cm (½in) round nozzle, and pipe 2.5–3cm (1–1¼in) round blobs onto the baking parchment, around 30 on each sheet. Phat and ting.

★ Bake the meringues in the oven for 1 hour or until they come away from the parchment. Turn the oven off and leave the baking sheet in the oven for 3–4 hours until cold as a can of ting and ting. Remove from the oven and set aside. The meringues can be stored in an airtight container for up to one week.

54

★ Heat 5cm (2in) water in a pan. Pop a heatproof bowl on top of the pan, making sure the bottom of the bowl is not touching the water. Place the chocolate in the bowl and let it melt easy now. Take the bowl off the heat and give the chocolate a stir to encourage any unmelted bits to melt in.

★ When ready to serve, spread a generous amount of melted chocolate on one pistachio meringue half, then sandwich together with another half. Continue to do this until all the halves are paired up. Serve immediately. Leave it now, fo' sho'.

HONEYCOMB MERINGUES

★ **Makes 10 pairs of chewy meringues**

★ **Take 2½ hours to make; plus cooling and drying (and 10 minutes to wash your mop out).**

A little vegetable oil
25g (1oz) granulated
   sugar
25g (1oz) toasted
   whole hazelnuts
3 large egg whites
150g (5oz) golden
   caster sugar
300ml (10fl oz) double
   cream
1–2 tbsp maple syrup
200g (7oz strawberries,
   halved if they are
   big boys

Praline is the joyous coupling of nuts and sugar, heated until it becomes toffee and then ground down quite finely. It lends a delicate crunch and a nutty depth to these amazing – though I say so myself – meringues. After much experimentation at Sugar HQ, a eureka moment produced a meringue with a chewy honeycomb centre. I have Joyce to thank for suggesting the novel addition of maple syrup to the cream. As a result Joyce has a 41% share in Hope and Greenwood for an investment of a tittle-over with a duster and a warm mop run over the kitchen.

★ First, make the praline. Line a baking sheet with baking parchment and brush with a little oil. Put the sugar and hazelnuts in a heavy-based pan and heat very gently until the sugar has dissolved, stirring with a wooden spoon. Cook for around 3 minutes, until the sugar turns dark golden, then pour the mixture as quick as sticks onto the oiled parchment and leave it to set. When it is cool, break it up into smallish chunks and whiz in a food processor (or coffee grinder if you are that sort) to a fine crumb.

★ Preheat the oven to 120°C/250°F/Gas ½. Whisk the egg whites in a spotlessly clean, grease-free bowl until stiff peaks form and you can safely turn the bowl upside down

P.T.O.

over your head (take care not to overbeat it). Add the sugar a spoonful at a time, whisking well between each addition, until it has dissolved into the egg white.

Give it a good whisk after the last spoonful has been added.

★ Line two baking sheets with baking parchment (not greaseproof paper, please, or they will stick, like Ginger to Rogers), then dot a little meringue mixture underneath each corner to stick the paper down onto the tray.

★ Fold three-quarters of the praline into the meringue mix, and use a spoon to blob 20 spoonfuls of the meringue onto the parchment. Sprinkle each meringue with a little of the remaining praline. Bake for 2 hours, until they come away from the parchment. Turn off the oven, and leave them in the oven overnight to dry out.

★ Store in an airtight container once cool (otherwise they'll go soft). See page 15 for more info on this.

★ Whip the double cream to soft peak stage and fold in the maple syrup. Sandwich the meringues with a spoonful of the cream, and serve immediately, alongside a bowl of strawberries.

JAMMIE HEARTS

This, my friends, is a joyous thing: a pimped Jammie Dodger, filled with buttercream and strawberry jam and sprinkled with crunchy pink sugar crystals. Apparently, Mr Doctor Who tried to convince the Daleks that a Jammie Dodger was the self-destruct button for the TARDIS. I tried to convince Mr Greenwood that the vacuum cleaner is a mystic chariot, which will transport him to a world of nubile nymphs carrying pies and beer, but he was distracted by Sarah Jane's hotpants.

★ Preheat the oven to 180°C/350°F/Gas 4. Generously grease two baking sheets.

★ Beat the butter and sugar in a bowl with a wooden spoon until the mixture looks pale, soft and creamy. Gradually add the egg and beat until the mixture looks soft and whipped.

★ Add the flour and baking powder and work it into the butter mixture. Bring together with your hands and knead into a dough.

★ Knead the dough briefly, then shape into a disc, wrap in clingfilm and chill for 15 minutes. Roll out the chilled dough on a lightly floured board to about 5mm (¼in) thickness. Cut out 16 hearts using an 8cm (3in) cutter, then cut out a small heart from the middle of 8 hearts using a 4cm (1½in) cutter (for both cutters, this is measuring from the point of the top of the heart to the bottom point). These will be the tops of the biscuit and the uncut hearts will be the bases. You may need to re-roll the dough once or twice.

★ Brush each heart biscuit with egg white, then sprinkle them with

P.T.O.

★ **Makes around 8 pimped biscuits**

★ **Take 45 minutes to make; plus chilling, and it only takes 2 minutes to hoover the living room, Mr Greenwood!**

125g (4½oz) softened unsalted butter, plus extra for greasing
125g (4½oz) golden caster sugar
1 medium egg, beaten, plus an egg white for glazing
225g (8oz) plain flour, sifted, plus extra to dust
2 tsp baking powder
Pink-coloured sugar, for sprinkling (please see the end of this book for stockists)

For the filling
25g (1oz) softened unsalted butter
75g (3oz) golden icing sugar
1 tsp vanilla extract
Splash of milk
8 generous tsp seedless strawberry jam

coloured sugar. Put on two baking sheets, spaced well apart, and chill for 15 minutes. Once chilled, bake in the oven for 12 minutes until just golden. You may need to cook the dough in two batches. Cool on a wire rack.

★ Make the buttercream filling. Beat the butter in a bowl until soft. Sift over half the icing sugar and the vanilla extract and work the icing sugar into the butter with a spoon. Continue to add the remaining icing sugar, a little at a time, then stir in a splash of milk to make the mixture soft and creamy.

★ When the biscuits are completely cool, put a small spoonful of jam in the middle each base, spread out with a knife over just half the biscuit. Cover the other half with a little buttercream. Top with a heart biscuit top. Repeat until you fill and top all the biscuits. These can be stored in an airtight container, unfilled, for up to three days. Once filled, they'll need to be exterminated within a day.

TARDIS THEFT
I read somewhere that the TARDIS was actually 'acquired' from the set of Dixon of Dock Green, which was being filmed next door. Yes, I know you are going to write to me.

PETTICOAT TAILS WITH LAVENDER AND HONEY

★ **Makes 8 pointy biscuits**

★ **Take 50 minutes to make; plus 30 minutes to gather some heather.**

125g (4½oz) softened unsalted butter, plus extra for greasing
150g (5oz) plain flour, plus extra to dust
25g (1oz) rice flour
40g (1½oz) golden caster sugar, plus extra for sprinkling
2 dried lavender heads, chopped

For the honey mascarpone
250g tub mascarpone
2 heaped tsp thick-set honey

I have long held the romantic notion that this lovely shortbread biscuit, enlivened with lavender and honey and known as a 'petticoat tail' was modelled on a wee Scottish story. Picture this if you will: a bonnie lass, wandering on the moors is suddenly caught in a craggy updraught. From beneath her lady kilt is spied the lacy edge of her petticoat, embroidered with sailing ships, a prayer in stitches for the safe return of her husband who has been at sea for longer than she cares to recall. Big sigh.

★ Preheat the oven to 180°C/350°F/Gas 4. Lightly grease a baking sheet.
★ Pop the butter, flour, rice flour and sugar in a large bowl and rub in the butter with your fingers until the mixture starts to look crumbly.
★ Pull the dried flowers off the lavender heads and crumble into the mixture. Knead the mixture until it squadges into a smooth dough. Bring it together with your hands and put on a lightly floured board. Shape and roll into a round shape about 1.5cm (¾in) thick and around 18cm (7in) in diameter. Stick it on the prepared baking sheet.
★ Crimp the edges, like a pasty, and bake in the oven for 30–40 minutes until lightly golden. Sprinkle liberally with sugar as soon as it comes out of the oven. Take a knife and mark the shortbread into eight wedges, and prick each wedge with a fork. Slide a palette knife (or fish slice, if you are utensily challenged) underneath the round – really carefully now – easy does it, and slide onto a wire rack to cool.
★ Fold the mascarpone and honey together in a bowl. Break the shortbread into pieces and serve with the mascarpone on the side.

BACK IN THE REAL WORLD
Petticoat tails are named from the French 'petitscotés', a pointed biscuit eaten with wine. Damn foreigners.

SEA SALT MILLIONAIRE'S SHORTBREAD

★ **Makes 25 squares**

★ **Takes 1 hour to make; plus cooling, and chilling in the 'cuzzi.**

For the shortbread
125g (4½oz) softened unsalted butter, plus extra for greasing
175g (6oz) plain flour
40g (1½oz) golden caster sugar
A pinch of salt

For the caramel filling
125g (4½oz) unsalted butter, chopped
75g (3oz) light muscovado sugar
397g can condensed milk
1 tsp sea salt, plus extra for sprinkling

For the chocolate topping
175g (6oz) dark chocolate, minimum 70% cocoa solids, broken into pieces
25g (1oz) unsalted butter
Edible gold leaf (optional – please see the end of this book for stockists)

In a land called Essex, where the mountains are made from caviar and the lakes are vajazzled with Swarovski crystals, squats a hideously ugly troll. One day while whittling a friendly face in a rotten cauliflower, he spies (with his good eye) a young maiden skipping through the meadow.

'Come hither young maiden,' he beseeches, waving his gnarled stumps.

And blow me down she does indeed come hither. The maiden is sweet and kind and feeds him morsels of sweet shortbread with extra oozy caramel and dark chocolate from her knapsack. A salty tear of affection rolls down her cheek and plip-plops onto the buttery biscuit.

Behold! Shazam! A single true tear has released our top-ugly chum from an evil curse! He is really a millionaire! Just look at him loaded down with posh cars and gold bling like Donald Trump or a scratch-card winner.

From that day forward we call this magic biscuit Sea Salt Millionaire's Shortbread.

★ Preheat the oven to 180°C/350°F/Gas 4. Grease and line the base and sides of a square 17cm (6½in) square tin with baking parchment.
★ To make the shortbread, sift the flour into a large bowl and add the sugar and salt. Stir together. Rub in the butter with your fingers until it starts to clump together and form a dough. Plonk the dough into the prepared tin and press it in, using the back of a spoon or *Hello!*

magazine to even it out. Bake for around 30 minutes, or until it has a golden spray tan. Leave to cool in the tin for 30 minutes.

★ To make the filling, whap the butter, sugar, condensed milk and salt into a pan and heat gently to dissolve the sugar and melt the butter. Bring it up to the boil and, stirring constantly, simmer gently for 5 minutes. The mix may spit a little so a wise cook might wish to lower their Chanel sunnies for protection. Spoon the caramel on top of the shortbread and set aside for 30 minutes to cool and firm up. Please take the opportunity to straighten your hair.

★ Now for the chocolate topping. Heat 5cm (2in) water in a pan. Pop a heatproof bowl on top of the pan, making sure the bottom of the bowl is not touching the water. Melt the dark chocolate and butter in the bowl – don't stir it, otherwise it may turn thick, rather than being born that way. When everything has melted, stick a spoon in and gently fold the butter and chocolate together. Pour on top of the cooled caramel to cover, and sprinkle with sea salt. Leave to cool in the tin, then chill for around 30 minutes to firm up.

★ Remove from the tin once firm, anoint with a little edible gold leaf, cut into squares and serve.

THE BAD NEWS
Obviously they get married because the maiden has always wanted a house with electric gates and a 'cuzzi, Babe. Unfortunately our hero, the millionaire, was still an ugly troll. Such is life, ladies.

MARMALADE CAKE WITH ICING

★ **Makes one loaf cake**

★ **Takes 1 hour 30 minutes to make, and 6 months to build an underground shed.**

125g (4½oz) softened
   unsalted butter, plus
   extra for greasing
Zest and juice of 1 small
   orange
1 tbsp whisky
2 tbsp fine-shred marmalade
125g (4½oz) golden caster
   sugar
2 medium eggs, beaten
150g (5oz) plain flour
1 tsp baking powder

For the whisky syrup
2 tbsp whisky
1 tbsp golden caster sugar

For the icing
40g (1½oz) white chocolate,
   broken into pieces
50g (2oz) softened
   unsalted butter
150g (5oz) golden icing
   sugar
25ml (1fl oz) double cream
Zest of ½ orange

Here are Bob and Jeff. They are best friends. They have a secret underground shed. Here they are debating the ingredients of this splendid, whisky-spiked marmalade cake with chocolate-orange icing. Jeff likes fine-shred marmalade, while Bob prefers a thick-cut version. Bob likes red pullovers; Jeff likes bottle green. Bob is showing Jeff the size of his hammer; Jeff is wondering how big the nail is.

★ Preheat the oven to 170°C/325°F/Gas 3. Grease and line the base and sides of a 450g loaf tin with greaseproof paper. Swish the orange zest, juice, whisky and marmalade together in a bowl, and set aside.

★ Beat together the butter and sugar in a large bowl until pale and creamy. Gradually beat in the eggs. Sift the flour and baking powder into the bowl and add the marmalade mixture. Stir together with a metal spoon. Scrape the mixture into the loaf tin and bake in the oven for 50 minutes, or until a skewer inserted into it comes out clean.

★ For the syrup, put the whisky and sugar in a pan with 2 tablespoons of boiling water and heat gently. Using a skewer, prod holes all over the cake, then pour the whisky syrup over. Leave the cake to cool in the tin for 10 minutes, then remove and cool on a wire rack.

★ Now for the icing. Heat 5cm (2in) water in a pan. Pop a heatproof bowl on top of the pan, making sure the bottom of the bowl is not touching the water. Melt the white chocolate gently. Set aside to cool.

★ Beat the butter and icing sugar in a bowl until soft and creamy. Gently fold the double cream into the melted white chocolate. Add to the butter mix along with the orange zest and fold together. Spread over the top of the cooled cake. Lick the bowl, and serve the cake.

CHERRY GENOA CAKE

Genoa – as any fool doth know – is in Italy, adjacent to the seaside where doth livest Chris Columbus. Behold a man who sailed about finding things that no one had lost, including cherries, which he spotted somewhere at the edge of the world where there are giant squid.

He did come ashore, and lo there were some cherry trees and OMG some fair waitresses on roller skates did come to him and feed him this golden Cherry Genoa Cake flecked with spiced cinnamon and island secrets. And he did eateth of the cake, in fact quite a bit of it because it was well tasty, and he falleth into a slumber. And behold! He did miss the last ship home.

★ Preheat the oven to 150°C/300°F/Gas 2. Grease and line the base and sides of a 12½cm (5in) round cake tin with greaseproof paper.
★ Drop the glacé cherries into a heatproof bowl and add the soured cherries. Cover with boiling water and soak for 10 minutes. Drain well. Nice job.
★ Dash the flour into a bowl, add both types of cherries and storm-toss together. Set aside.
★ Beat the butter, sugar and cinnamon in a bowl until pale, soft and creamy, then gradually beat in the eggs. If it looks like the mixture is curdling; just throw in a smidge of flour (minus the cherries) to help bring it back together.
★ Fold in the remaining flour and cherry mixture, the baking powder and ground almonds. Spoon into the prepared tin, sprinkle over the flaked almonds and sugar crystals and bake in the oven for 1 hour 15 minutes, or until a skewer inserted in the centre comes out clean.
★ Slip the cake out of the tin and cool, then slice and munch.

★ Cuts into 8 golden slices

★ Takes 1 hour 35 minutes to make, and three years to sail to the edge of the world.

100g (4oz) softened unsalted butter, plus extra for greasing
100g (4oz) glacé cherries, quartered
50g (2oz) soured cherries, halved
100g (4oz) plain flour, sifted
100g (4oz) golden caster sugar
¼ tsp ground cinnamon
2 large eggs, beaten
1 tsp baking powder
50g (2oz) ground almonds
10g (¼oz) flaked almonds
Sugar crystals, to sprinkle (please see the end of this book for stocklsts)

HISTORICAL FACT
CC also discovered microwave chips, tummy-button fluff and roller skates.

TOP-NOTCH CHOCOLATE TRUFFLE CAKE

★ **Cuts into 12 slices**

★ **Takes just under 2 hours to make**

275ml (9½ fl oz) vegetable
  oil, plus extra for greasing
400g (14oz) light
  muscovado sugar
400g (14oz) plain flour
2 tsp baking powder
a pinch of salt
100g (4oz) cocoa powder
275ml (10fl oz) water
2 medium eggs
2tsp red wine vinegar
1 tsp vanilla

For the filling, icing and decoration

225g (8oz) dark chocolate,
  minimum 50% cocoa
  solids, very finely chopped
300ml (10fl oz) double cream
2 tbsp icing sugar, or more,
  to taste
6 tbsp blackcurrant jam
Two handfuls of small
  blackberries, halved
A handful of Hope and
  Greenwood Best of
  British truffles

Here at the Rosey O'Conner's exercise class, thunder thighs Doreen is thrilling us with some lunges. Disaster strikes as Doreen is felled by a Lycra wedgie. Luckily she can console herself with this calorie-free chocolate cake.

★ Please preheat the oven to 180°C/350°F/Gas 4. Grease and line a deep 18cm (7 inch) round cake tin with greaseproof paper. The paper should come a centimetre above the edge.

★ Put all the ingredients for the cake into a bowl and whisk until everything is well blended.

★ Spoon the mixture into the tin and bake for 2 hours or until a skewer inserted into the centre comes out clean. Cool in the tin for 10 minutes, then remove and leave to cool on a wire rack.

★ Remove the greaseproof paper, then slice off the domed top using a bread knife to make it level. Slice the cake carefully into three even layers horizontally.

★ Now make the icing. Place the chocolate in a bowl. Pour the cream into a pan and add the sugar. Bring it up to the boil, then turn off the heat. Pour the cream over the chocolate and stir to mix together and make a smooth icing. Set aside to cool and thicken.

★ Spread half the jam over two of the cake layers then put the blackberries on top of the jam. When the icing is cool enough, spread a little over each fruit layer, then put the cake together.

★ Take around a third of the icing mixture and spread it over the top of the cake. Take another third and smooth around half of the side. Do the same with the rest of the icing to cover the other half. Arrange the truffles on the top of the cake and serve.

Simple
Slimming
by Ann Seymour
and diets for beauty

SQUIRREL GREENWOOD'S SPLENDID FRUIT CAKE

★ Styles out into
8 slices

★ Takes 1 hour
50 minutes to make;
plus overnight soaking,
and 10 minutes to
practise your hippety-
hoppity moves.

75g (3oz) currants
75g (3oz) sultanas
75g (3oz) raisins
50g (2oz) dried apricots,
   chopped
40g (1½oz) lemon
   candied peel, chopped
200ml (7fl oz) hot black
   tea, made with 1
   Earl Grey tea bag
75g (3oz) unsalted butter,
   plus extra for greasing
75g (3oz) soft light brown
   sugar
125g (4½oz) plain flour
2 tsp baking powder
1 tsp mixed spice
1 large egg, beaten
A handful of roasted
   salted almonds, to
   decorate

Deep, deep, deep in the Dark Wood, would-be gangsta Squirrel Greenwood sets off to find some scrummy fruit and nuts for his rather splendid Fruit Cake.

Wood Pigeon warns Weasel, and Weasel warns Mouse,
   'Squirrel Greenwood is coming, he is coming!'
The reeds at the river's edge whisper,
   'Over the bridge, over the bridge.'
The wind in the trees sings,
   'Through the gate, through the gate.'
The Great Lord of the Green rattles his leaves and looms darkly from his moss-soft slumber,
   'Squirrel Greenwood, you dare visit this bewitched place?' he booms, 'Be gone! For tonight when the moon shines on Acorn Hill and the fairy folk slide the slippery Maypole, the Itchy Pixie will be waiting perchance to mess you up.'
   'Wagwan,' says Squirrel Greenwood and hooks up with MC Badger up for some hippety-hoppity practice.

★ Put the fruit and peel in a sealable container and pour over the hot tea. Cover it and leave it to cuddle up overnight. The tea will have soaked into the fruit by the following morning. You get me?
★ The next day, preheat the oven to 150°C/300°F/Gas 2. Grease and line the base and sides of a 12.5cm (5in) round cake tin with greaseproof paper. Wicked.

72

★ Melt the butter and sugar in a pan. Cool.

★ Sift the flour, baking powder and mixed spice into a large bowl. Plop in the soaked fruit and toss it about to mix. Slop in the melted butter and sugar, fo'shizzle, and the egg. Give everything a vigorous stir to check there are no floury bits.

★ Spoon the cake mixture into the prepared tin and bake in the oven for 1 hour 30 minutes, taking the opportunity to pick the cat hairs off your hoodie. After 30 minutes, gently push the almonds on top in a jolly pattern and continue to bake until a skewer inserted into the centre of the cake comes out clean. Cool the cake in the tin, then remove and serve.

★ The cake will keep well wrapped in clingfilm and stored in a sealable container for up to five days. And that's how I roll.

DOCTOR'S NOTE
I am beginning to question Miss Hope's sanity, this has gone beyond codeine.

STICKY TOFFEE AND GINGER CAKE

Nurse Brenda often finds herself in sticky situations. While extolling the virtues of Doctor Luder's Sticky Toffee and Ginger Cake, the sweetness of the dates, the richness of the molasses, the bite of ginger, isn't this cupboard cramped, Doctor etc., she inadvertently dribbled toffee all down her newly starched utility overall.

★ Drop the dates in a bowl with the bicarbonate of soda and 150ml (5fl oz) boiling water. Leave to soak for 10 minutes. Straighten your apron.

★ Preheat the oven to 190°C/375°F/Gas 5. Grease a 20cm (8in) round cake tin and line the base and sides with greaseproof paper. There is no need for rubber gloves unless the mood takes you.

★ Beat the molasses sugar and butter in a bowl with vigour and vim until the mixture looks slightly paler and creamy, and beat in the eggs. It will look like gritty sand but don't fret dear friend, it will come together beautifully with the flour.

★ Sift the flour, baking powder and ginger over the mixture and fold everything together, adding the soaked dates and grated stem ginger. Spoon it into the prepared tin and bake for 30 minutes, or until a skewer inserted into the centre of the cake comes out clean. Turn out of the tin and leave to cool on a wire rack.

★ When you are ready to serve the cake, heat the double cream and sugar in a small pan until the sugar dissolves. Bring the mixture

P.T.O.

★ **Serves 8–10**

★ **Takes 1 hour to make; plus 10 minutes soaking and 10 minutes how's-your-father in the store room.**

100g (4oz) dried, pitted dates, chopped
½ tsp bicarbonate of soda
125g (4½oz) molasses sugar
125g (4½oz) unsalted butter
2 medium eggs
225g (8oz) self-raising flour
2 tsp baking powder
2 tsp ground ginger
2 balls stem ginger in syrup, drained and grated

For the toffee sauce
300ml (12fl oz) double cream
100g (4oz) light muscovado sugar
A good squeeze of lemon juice
A pinch of sea salt

up to the boil, stirring well, and simmer for 2–3 minutes until thickened. Stir in the lemon juice and salt.

★ Put the cake on a serving plate, and drizzle over a little of the sticky toffee sauce. Pour the remaining sauce into a little jug and serve on the side.

Aversion Therapy

To avoid you dribbling toffee sauce all down your apron, I'm serving my toffee sauce on the side, just how Nurse Brenda likes it.

PEAR AND CHOCOLATE TRIFLE

★ **Serves 6 sensible people, or just me**

★ **Takes 55 minutes to make; plus chilling, and 30 minutes on my exercise bike.**

2 just-ripe pears
150ml (5fl oz) ruby port
1 tbsp golden caster sugar
125g (4½oz) chocolate cake (you could use the leftovers from the Top-notch Chocolate Truffle Cake on page 70), roughly crumbled
1 medium egg yolk
1 tbsp cornflour
4 tsp golden caster sugar
225ml (8fl oz) milk
1 tbsp cocoa powder
20g (¾oz) dark chocolate, broken into pieces
200ml (7fl oz) double cream
2 tsp icing sugar

For the popping candy decoration
25g (1oz) dark chocolate, broken into pieces
Sachet of Fizz Wiz popping candy, or edible glitter

I have spent today having my soul captured via a camera for a well-known magazine. I've been primped, pulled and tweaked (I quite liked the tweaked bit).

'Stop slouching,' said the photographer, 'you look like Miss Piggy!'

I have had to console myself with some rich port-laced Pear and Chocolate Trifle, thrilled with popping candy. Two helpings, actually.

★ First up let's make the popping candy decoration because I know you want to. Please melt the chocolate in a small bowl over a pan of simmering water, making sure the base doesn't touch the bottom. When it has melted, use a teaspoon to shape six popping chocolate hearts, wiggles or amoebas on a sheet of baking parchment. Sprinkle over the popping candy or edible glitter. Leave them alone to set.

★ Peel and halve the pears, and put them in a small pan. Pour in 200ml (7fl oz) water and the port, and sprinkle over the sugar. Cover them with a scrunched-up then pulled-out sheet of greaseproof paper, then put a lid on the pan. Thank you. Bring to the boil, turn the heat down low and simmer for 15–20 minutes, turning them over halfway through, until the pears are tender when pierced with a sharp knife. Take them out of the syrup and cool them.

★ Keep the juice in the pan, bring it up to the boil and simmer for 5 minutes to reduce to a lovely sticky yumminess.

P.T.O.

★ Remove the stems and cores from the pear halves and chop into small cubes. Divide between six pretty 150ml (5fl oz) trifle glasses, or pop the cubes into one large glass serving dish. Crown with some of the crumbled cake, then pour the pear syrup over the top.

★ Now for the custard. Mix the egg yolk, cornflour and sugar in a bowl with a sploosh of milk. Stir in the cocoa powder. Scald the milk – pour it into a pan and bring to the boil. Turn off the heat as soon as bubbles appear around the edge. Pour the hot milk over the egg mixture, stirring well. Rinse out the pan, then return the mixture to the pan with the chocolate and gently bring to the boil, stirring all the time, cooking the mixture for 3–4 minutes until thickened and custard-like. Get a whisk in there if you think it needs it.

★ Spoon the custard over the chocolate cake and pop the trifles (or trifle) in the fridge for about 30 minutes to set. You can do everything up to this bit up to a day ahead, if you are a swot.

★ Whisk the double cream and icing sugar together in a bowl until soft peaks form and it's just holding its shape. Spoon on top of the trifle, and spread to cover, then decorate with a chocolate popping heart, et voila.

BRANDY SNAPS WITH SPICED MANDARIN CREAM

★ **Makes 12 magic brandy snaps**

★ **Take 45 minutes to make, and 10 minutes to lay a round table.**

25g (1oz) unsalted butter, plus extra for greasing
25g (1oz) golden caster sugar
1 tbsp golden syrup
25g (1oz) plain flour
¼ tsp ground ginger
1 tsp brandy

For the spiced mandarin cream
1 mandarin
100ml (4fl oz) double cream
1 tbsp golden icing sugar
½ tsp ground ginger
Whole nutmeg, for grating

Piping bag and nozzle

King Arthur of Camelot was playing a fraught game of hide-and-seek with Lady Gwynny of the Lake. Shattered, they flopped onto their beanbags. Luckily, Mr Merlin magicked up some delicious brandy snaps laced with real brandy and filled with a mischievous cream peppered with nutmeg and mandarins.

'Magic!' said King Arthur to Mr Merlin, 'You may kiss my ring.'

★ Waste no time my friend and preheat the oven to 180°C/350°F/ Gas 4. Please heat the butter, sugar and syrup over a low heat in a small pan until the sugar has dissolved. Sift over the flour and ginger, then add the brandy and stir everything together. Magic.

★ Now put the mixture to one side for a minute, while you line two baking trays with baking parchment. Kindly spoon six small blobettes of mixture onto each tray, spaced well apart, and bake them for six minutes. Each blob will have spread out into a lacy round and will be pale golden. Special tip: Bake one tray at a time, otherwise the biscuits will harden on the trays for too long and you won't be able to roll them all up.

★ Now for the fun bit. Grease three wooden spoons well with butter. When the biscuits come out of the oven, wait for them to stop bubbling and for them to flatten onto the tray. Working quickly, wrap each one around each handle, using a palette knife or table knife to help lift them from the tray. Wait a few seconds until they firm up, then slide off and leave to set on a wire rack. Handy hint: if the biscuits get too hard to roll, pop them back in the oven for a few seconds.

★ Bake the other tray and roll those biscuits, too.

★ Without any further a-do, zest the mandarin, then peel the segments and chop them up. Whip the cream in a bowl until just thick. Fold in the icing sugar, ground ginger and chopped mandarin and zest, and a good grating of nutmeg. Spoon it into a piping bag fitted with a 1cm (½in) fluted nozzle and pipe into the ends of each brandy snap.

Footnote

'Where,' says King Lord Arthur to Lady Gwynny of the Lake, 'did I hide that holy grail?'

CUTE BERRY TARTS

This morning I came downstairs to find the bears and all their bear chums crashed on my sofa again, with pizza boxes festering on the occasional table, and shoes like boats moored in the hall. They have devoured the cute berry tarts I made for tea. Darn bears, there's crème patissière smeared on the poof and raspberry handprints up the dado. Those bears drive me crazy, why do they slob out all day doing nothing? They need to get a job. I'm going to stop doing their laundry, that will show them.

★ Put the butter and icing sugar in a bowl and beat with a wooden spoon until pale, soft and creamy. Then add the egg yolk and continue to beat in until all smushed together. Sift the flour into the bowl and work the mixture to make a dough. Bring the mix together with your hands, wrap it in clingfilm and chill for about 30 minutes.
★ Now roll out the chilled dough on a lightly floured board to a 3mm thickness then cut out squares of pastry to fit eight tiny tart tins. Gently press the pastry into each tin, and carefully trim any excess. Thank you, most kind. Freeze for 10 minutes. This will help to set the pastry so it doesn't shrink in the tin, that would mean less tart and that would be most undesirable. Preheat the oven to 200°C/400°F/Gas 6.
★ Remove the tart tins from the freezer. Prick each tart base with a fork and line with a scrunched up piece of greaseproof paper and baking beans, then put on a baking sheet and bake in the oven for around 5–8 minutes until just dry on the base. Remove the

P.T.O.

★ **Makes 8 tiny little tarts (If you are feeling flush, buy 16 tins and double the recipe.)**

★ **Take 40 minutes to make; plus chilling, and 10 minutes to stop the bears' pocket money.**

20g (¾oz) softened unsalted butter
1 tsp icing sugar
½ medium egg yolk, mixed with 1 tsp cold water
40g (1½oz) plain flour, plus extra to dust
Summer fruit, such as raspberries, blackberries, strawberries and blueberries
1–2 tbsp seedless strawberry jam

For the custard filling
½ medium egg yolk
7g (¼oz) golden caster sugar
7g (¼oz) cornflour and plain flour, mixed
75ml (3fl oz) milk
¼ tsp vanilla extract
1 tbsp double cream

8 tiny petit four tart tins (please see the end of this book for stockists)
Piping bag and nozzle (optional)

greaseproof paper and beans, and return to the oven for around 2 minutes. Leave the pastry to cool in the tins for a few minutes, then remove carefully with a small palette knife and cool on a wire rack. Have a lie down, the worst is over.

★ Now let's make the filling. Mix together the egg yolk, sugar and flours. Sploosh the milk into a small pan and bring just to the boil. Pour the milk and vanilla extract over the egg mixture and stir together. Pour the mixture back into the pan and cook over a low heat, stirring all the time, until thickened. Spoon the custard into a bowl, cover with clingfilm and cool.

★ Next up, heat the strawberry jam in a small pan with one teaspoon of water until lovely and runny. Tip the runny jam into a bowl and cool.

★ Mix the double cream into the custard filling, and spoon a dollop into each pastry case (or pipe it prettily using a piping bag fitted with a 1cm/½in round nozzle). Arrange some fresh fruit of your choice on top and spoon over the jam to glaze the fruit and the filling. Serve immediately. Totally yummy.

TREACLE TARTS

Anyone worth their Toot Sweets will know that it was treacle tart that the childcatcher used in Chitty Chitty Bang Bang to lure the children out of their houses. My phantasmagorical version made with golden syrup, a hint of lemon and a sprinkle of nutmeg has a golden lattice criss-cross pastry top. Guaranteed to lure ladies out of Selfridges Shoe Lounge. Ok, that's possibly a stretch of the imagination.

★ Put the plain flour into a food processor and add the butter and salt. Whiz until the mixture looks like fine breadcrumbs. Add a tablespoon of water and whiz again until it just starts to come together. If it looks a bit dry, drizzle in a teaspoon or two more of water.

★ Tip out onto a board, bring together with your hands and knead lightly to bring the dough together. Wrap in clingfilm and chill for 15 minutes. This helps the pastry to relax and prevents it from shrinking when rolling out.

★ Preheat the oven to 200°C/400°F/Gas 6. Remove the pastry from the fridge, unwrap and roll it out on a lightly floured board until it's about 2mm thick. Use to line six tins, reserving the remainder (wrap and chill this bit as you'll need it later for the lattice topping). Prick the bases a couple of times with a fork and put in the freezer for 10 minutes to chill quickly. There's no need to cover them.

★ Remove the tart tins from the freezer, line each with a small piece of baking parchment that's been scrunched up and pulled apart again,

★ **Makes 6**

★ **Take 1 hour 20 minutes to make; plus chilling and freezing.**

150g (5oz) plain flour, sifted, plus extra to dust
75g (3oz) chilled unsalted butter, cubed
A pinch of salt
125g (4½oz) golden syrup
50g (2oz) breadcrumbs
Zest from ¼ unwaxed lemon and a good squeeze of juice
Whole nutmeg, for grating
Golden caster sugar, for sprinkling

Six 8cm (3in) shallow tart tins

P.T.O.

and fill them with baking beans. Put on a baking sheet and bake in the oven for 10 minutes. Remove the paper and beans and return the tart cases to the oven to cook for a further 1–2 minutes, until the pastry looks dry (lift the parchment from one of the pastry cases to check). When it does, remove the tins from the oven and set aside to cool while you make the filling.

★ Increase the oven temperature to 220°C/425°F/Gas 7. Warm the golden syrup in a pan over a low heat until it runs freely, then stir in the breadcrumbs, lemon zest, lemon juice and enough nutmeg for it to taste just a little bit spicy. Spoon into the pastry cases.

★ Roll out the remaining pastry on a lightly floured board and cut it into 5mm strips, long enough to fit across the tart tins – you'll need six for each tart. Place on top of the filled tarts, weaving them through each other so that you create a lattice pattern. Trim off any loose ends, and pinch them into the pastry edge. Brush the strips with water and sprinkle with sugar.

★ Bake in the oven for 15–20 minutes until golden. Serve warm or cold.

PS
'Treacle tart' is Cockney rhyming slang for 'sweetheart', as in 'Fancy a ride in my new car, treacle?'

LITTLE APPLE STRUDELS

★ **Makes 16 wunderbar morsels**

★ **Take 45 minutes to make and 20 minutes to squeeze into your lederhosen.**

40g (1 ½oz) unsalted
    butter
1 small slice white or
    wholemeal bread
1 small Bramley apple –
    around 250g (9oz) –
    peeled, cored and finely
    chopped
2 tbsp sultanas
Zest of ½ lemon
1 tbsp light muscovado
    sugar
A good pinch of ground
    cinnamon
A good pinch of mixed
    spice
Four 25 x 50cm (10 x 20in)
    sheets ready-made filo
    pastry
Icing sugar, to dust
Double cream, to serve

Once upon a time in the Black Forest there was a master baker called Johannes. Johannes harvested apples to make his world-famous Apple Strudel. His comely wife Helga added sultanas, cinnamon and spices, and wrapped the fragrant mixture in crisp filo pastry. Folk came from miles around for Kaffee & Kuchen. Unfortunately, while crossing the bridge to market, Johannes was eaten by a troll who didn't like the cut of his lederhosen.

★ Preheat the oven to 200°C/400°F/Gas 6. Melt the butter in a pan over a low heat, strain through a sieve and into a bowl to remove the white crusty top. Set aside to cool.
★ Cut the crusts off the bread, chop roughly and whiz in a food processor to make breadcrumbs. Tip into a bowl. Add the apple, sultanas, lemon zest, sugar and spices and mix everything together.
★ Lay a sheet of filo pastry on a board, with the longest length along the bottom. Cut it into four vertically, so you have four long thin rectangles.
★ Brush the long edge of one strip with melted butter, then spoon about 1 tablespoon of the apple mixture onto the bottom of the strip. Roll the pastry around the filling, tucking in the sides as you go. Brush again with melted butter, then put on a baking sheet. Do the same with the remaining pastry and filo to make 16 rolls.
★ Bake in the oven for 15 minutes until golden. Dust with icing sugar and serve warm with cream.

CHOCOLATE AND REDCURRANT MILLEFEUILLES

★ **Makes 9 many-layered pastries**

★ **Take 55 minutes to make and 8–10 minutes to shower off the chocolate cream.**

½ x 425g pack ready-rolled puff pastry
Plain flour, to dust

For the chocolate cream filling
1 medium egg yolk
1 tbsp golden caster sugar
1 tbsp cornflour
1 tbsp drinking chocolate
150ml (5fl oz) milk
4 tbsp double cream

For the decoration
75g (3oz) white icing sugar
1 tsp cocoa powder
9 sprigs of redcurrants

Piping bag and 1cm (½in) nozzle

Jean, next-door nudist and thoughtful housewife, pipes her magnificent pastries with rich chocolate cream and decorates them with sprigs of redcurrants and a light dusting of icing sugar. On a sunny Sunday I often spot her treating Mr G over the garden fence. Then she turns her attention to the millefeuilles.

★ Please preheat the oven to 220°C/425°F/Gas 7. Roll out the pastry on a lightly floured board until it measures 23.5 x 26cm (9 x 10in). Now tidy the edges to make a perfect rectangle measuring 22.5 x 23.5cm (8¾ x 9½in). Cut out 18 rectangles, each measuring around 2.5 x 11.5cm (1 x 4½in). Prick them all over with a fork, then place them on a baking sheet and bake in the oven for 8–10 minutes until risen and just golden. Remove from the oven and leave to cool on a wire rack. Now for a cheat: Once the pastry slices are cool, use a small sharp knife to slice between the horizontal layers of each piece and separate them into two – four layers will make one millefeuille. I won't tell a soul.

★ Place the egg yolk, sugar, cornflour and drinking chocolate in a small bowl and stir in a splash of milk. Put the rest of the milk in a small pan and bring to the boil, then pour it onto the cornflour mixture. Stir the gloop well to mix together. Return the mixture to the pan, bring to the boil and simmer for a couple of minutes, stirring all the time, until thickened. Nice action. Spoon into a bowl, cover with clingfilm (this stops a skin from forming on the top) and cool.

★ Mix the icing sugar in a bowl with a drop of water until putty-like.

★ Now we can build the pastry. Spoon the chocolate cream into the piping bag, fitted with a 1cm (½in) round nozzle. Please be so kind as to arrange four layers of pastry in piles on a board – that's nine piles. Take layer one and pipe the chocolate cream onto the pastry, place the second layer of pastry on top. Pipe the cream onto the second layer, and repeat with the third layer (you can use a spoon, but piping is by far the best and prettiest method). Leave the top layer without the cream. Fill all the millefeuilles like this.

★ For the tops, spoon over the white icing to cover. Add the teaspoon of cocoa powder to the remaining icing in the bowl and add a dash more water to loosen the mixture. Drizzle it over the white icing to create a pattern, or pipe it on top using a small fine nozzle. Leave to set, then put on top of the sandwiched millefeuille and decorate each with a redcurrant sprig.

BLUEBERRY BAKEWELLS WITH LEMON SYLLABUB

Well, say 'hello' to plump blueberries nestling in frangipane with a stonking lemon syllabub laced with sweet wine on the side. London's finest bus conductress and Grandad's first love, Betty Bright, fell in love with Harold Bowden, on the number 13 bus to Tottenham Court Road. As the bus careered around Eros, she 'accidentally' sat on his cherry bakewells.

'Ooh cherry bakewells,' flushed Betty, 'I don't mind if I do.'

★ Makes 8 old-school tarts

★ Take 45 minutes; plus chilling and cooling and 30 seconds to motor around Eros on a bus.

40g (1½oz) chilled
   unsalted butter, cubed
2 tsp golden caster sugar
85g (3½oz) plain flour,
   sifted, plus extra to dust

★ Put the butter, sugar and flour in a food processor and whiz until the mixture resembles breadcrumbs. Drizzle over 1–2 teaspoons of cold water and whiz again until the mixture just starts to come together. Marvellous. Tip the mix onto a board and bring it together with your hands. Knead it very lightly – don't overwork it, otherwise the finished pastry will be tough – until it comes together in a ball, then shape into a flat disc, wrap it in greaseproof paper and chill for 10 minutes. That's the ticket.

☛ P.T.O.   FOR MORE INGREDIENTS AND RECIPE METHOD

For the frangipane filling

40g (1½oz) softened unsalted butter

40g (1½oz) golden caster sugar

2 tbsp beaten egg

40g (1½oz) ground almonds

4 level tsp plain flour

A handful of blueberries (three for each tart)

Golden icing sugar, to dust

For the lemon syllabub

½ tsp lemon zest

1½ tbsp sweet dessert wine

125ml (4½fl oz) double cream

2 tsp icing sugar

Eight 6cm (2½in) mini fluted deep tart tins

★ Divide the pastry into eight pieces (it doesn't look like much but, I promise, you only need a wee bit) and roll each piece out on a lightly floured board to fit each tart tin. It'll be around 2–3mm thick. Use a disc of pastry to line each tin. Prick the bases with a fork and freeze for 10 minutes. There is no need to cover them unless you think someone might sit on them..

★ Turn the oven to 200°C/400°F/Gas 6 as you'll soon be ready to bake the tarts. For the frangipane filling, beat the butter and sugar together in a small bowl until pale, soft and creamy. Add the egg and have another jolly good go at beating the mixture together. Fold in the ground almonds and flour. Divide the filling equally among the eight frozen pastry cases. Top with the blueberries, pushing them gently into the filling. Place the tart tins on a baking sheet and bake in the oven for 20–25 minutes until delicious and golden. Cool in the tin for 10 minutes, then remove and cool completely on a wire rack.

★ Now you can make the syllabub. Whisk all the ingredients together in a bowl until thickened and softly whipped. Serve with the tarts. Well thank you, I don't mind if I do.

Broken heart
All Grandad was left with were his memories and the sheet music for 'She Wears Red Feathers' (and a hoolie-hoolie skirt).

ORANGE CUSTARD TARTS

Live! This evening! The Belvoir Club presents to you the bouncy, the baby-oiled, the breathtaking Janice la Floof and her Chicken in a Basquette routine. Chicken juggling corsetry! Egg smuggling hosiery! Orange custard tart-ping-pong! Free steak pie with every pint!

She's a great girl, my daughter.

★ Place the butter, sugar and flour in a food processor, and whiz until the mixture looks like breadcrumbs. Drizzle over 1–2 teaspoons of cold water and whiz again until the mixture just starts to come together. Tip the mix onto a board and bring it together with your hands. Knead it very lightly – don't overwork it, otherwise the finished pastry will be tough – until it comes together in a ball, then shape into a flat disc, wrap in greaseproof paper and chill for 10 minutes.

★ Preheat the oven to 180°C/350°F/Gas 4. Divide the pastry into eight pieces (it doesn't look like much but, I promise, you only need a little bit) and roll each piece out on a lightly floured board to fit each tart. It'll be around 2–3mm thick. Use to line each tart tin. Prick the bases with a fork and freeze for 10 minutes. There is no need to cover them, unless you think something will fall on top of them, like your juggling chickens.

★ Line each pastry case with a small piece of baking parchment, which has been scrunched up and pulled apart again. Fill with baking beans, then place on a baking sheet and blind bake in the oven for 10 minutes.

P.T.O.

★ **Makes 8 cheeky tarts**

★ **Take around 1 hour to make; plus chilling and freezing. And 10 minutes to retrieve the eggs.**

40g (1½oz) chilled unsalted butter, cubed
2 tsp golden caster sugar
85g (3½oz) plain flour

For the custard filling
40g (1½oz) beaten egg
40g (1½oz) golden caster sugar
Zest of ¼ orange, and a good squeeze of juice
40ml (1½fl oz) double cream

For the decoration
8 small orange segments, skinned and pith removed
A little golden caster sugar

Eight 6cm (2½in) mini fluted deep tart tins

BLACKC...
Put blackcurran...
heat until the juice runs. ...
into baked pastry case. Thicken...
with 1 teaspoon Bird's Custard ...
pour over fruit. Cover when cold...
Bird's delicious whipped Custard.

ORANGE CUSTARD PIE
Make up 1 pint extra-thick Bird's Custard,
add the juice and grated rind of one orange.
When cool, pour into baked and cooled
pastry case and leave to set. Decorate top
with orange sections and whipped custard.

Bird's Custard

BIRD'S
CUSTARD
POW...

★ Remove the paper and beans and return to the oven for 1–2 minutes for the pastry to dry out. Excellent work. Please take the tarts out of the oven and put them aside to cool a little. Turn down the oven to 150°C/300°F/Gas 2.

★ Pop the egg, sugar, orange zest, orange juice and cream into a bowl. then stir with a wooden spoon. Carefully divide the creamy mixture equally among the pastry cases.

★ Pop the tarts back on the baking sheet, and bake in the oven for 15 minutes, or until the custard has set. Remove the little lovelies from the oven and cool on a wire rack.

★ To finish off, please put the oranges on a baking sheet and sprinkle with sugar. Use a kitchen blowtorch to scorch each of them (or blast them under a hot grill), then put a segment on top of each tart and serve.

HAZELNUT TARTS WITH STRAWBERRIES

This recipe for hazelnut biscuits layered with strawberries and cream comes courtesy of Granny Hope, who often made this for her am' dram' parties as one large 'galette', as she calls it. She also had a banquette, a breakfast bar and a hostess trolley, a grapefruit segmenter, grape scissors and an egg coddler.

★ Preheat the oven to 200°C/400°F/Gas 6. Line a large baking sheet with baking parchment.

★ Toast the hazelnuts in the oven for 5 minutes until golden. Cool the nuts completely, then put them in a food processor with the icing sugar and whiz until coarsely chopped. Now add the flour, salt and butter and whiz until the mixture resembles breadcrumbs. Top marks.

★ Add the egg yolk and blitz until the mixture just comes together. Tip it onto a board and bring together with your hands. Wrap the dough in baking parchment and chill for 15 minutes until firm.

★ Unwrap the dough and leave it sitting on the baking parchment. Dust your rolling pin and the surface of the dough with flour, and roll it out (on the parchment) to a 5mm thickness. Cut out 24 rounds using a 4cm (1½in) round cutter, re-rolling when necessary. Prick each round all over, then transfer to the prepared baking sheet and bake for 8–10 minutes until golden. Cool on a wire rack.

★ Beat the mascarpone and icing sugar together in a bowl. Chill it for half an hour so it firms up. Spoon it into a piping bag, fitted with a 1cm (½in) star nozzle, and pipe a swirl onto all the pastry rounds. Put two halves together, and top each tart with more cream and a strawberry.

★ **Makes 12 Granny Hope specials**

★ **Take 30 minutes to make, plus chilling and 5 minutes to pop on Manuel and his 'Music of the Mountains' and your kaftan.**

50g (2oz) whole blanched hazelnuts
25g (1oz) icing sugar, plus extra to dust
40g (1½oz) plain flour, plus extra to dust
A pinch of salt
40g (1½oz) chilled unsalted butter, cubed, plus extra to grease
1 medium egg yolk, beaten

For the decoration
250g tub mascarpone
3 tbsp icing sugar
12 small strawberries (if they're larger, halve or quarter them as necessary)

Piping bag and 1cm (½in) star nozzle

CHURROS WITH CHOCOLATE SAUCE

★ **Makes around 16, but can we make more – yes?**

★ **Take 40 minutes to make. Not sure I can wait that long actually.**

25g (1oz) golden caster sugar, plus extra for sprinkling
1 tbsp vegetable oil
75g (3oz) plain flour, sifted
1–2 litres (1¾–3½ pints) vegetable oil, for deep-frying
Golden caster sugar, for sprinkling
Ground cinnamon, for sprinkling

For the chocolate sauce
100ml (4fl oz) double cream
Good splash of sweet sherry or Cointreau
50g (2oz) dark chocolate, minimum 60% cocoa solids, broken into pieces

Piping bag and 1cm (½in) star nozzle
Scissors

If I were you, I wouldn't make this recipe for a Spanish donut known as a churro. Why bother with piping fresh hot donuts? Why stretch yourself to sprinkling them with sparkling sugar and cinnamon? Personally, I wouldn't give kitchen space to the thick, thick, hot chocolate made with cream and flavoured with Cointreau. Total rubbish recipe. Really, seriously, don't bother, there is nothing for you here, jog on.

★ Put l 25ml (4½fl oz) water in a small pan with the sugar and oil. Bring the liquid to the boil, then turn off the heat and add the flour immediately. Stir vigorously until the mixture comes together in a ball. Oh, it's so exciting.

★ Heat the oil for deep-frying in a large frying pan. It will be ready when a cube of bread turns golden in about 30 seconds. Spoon the mixture into a piping bag fitted with a l cm (½in) star nozzle. I'm getting all giddy now.

★ Squeeze 5cm (2in) lengths of the churros mixture directly into the hot oil, snipping them off at the nozzle with scissors as you go. Add four or five donut sausages to the pan at a time, depending on how big it is. They'll draw together like Fred and Ginger but they'll be easy to separate once they have a bit of colour. Fry for 2–3 minutes, until they are dark golden and crisp on the outside, then lift out with a slotted spoon and drain on a plate lined with kitchen paper. Jumpy, jumpy around my kitchen!

★ Please soldier on until you've cooked all the mixture. Sprinkle the sausages with caster sugar and cinnamon. SQUEAL. Dribble a bit.

★ Pour the cream and sherry (or Cointreau) into a pan and bring to the boil. Take the pan off the heat and add the chocolate. Stir gently until the chocolate has melted. Try and control yourself. Take a churro and dunk it in the chocolate. Have a lie down and try to remember when was the last time anything so bad tasted this good.

BETTER THINGS
TO DO THAN MAKE
CHURROS:
Watch a banana take a nap
Speed-date a slow lorris
Chat to a door knob

MOCHA ECLAIRS

★ **Makes 16 adorable little pastries**

★ **Take 50 minutes to make; plus setting time, and 25 years in a high security prison.**

65ml (2½ fl oz) milk
20g (¾oz) chilled unsalted
    butter, cubed
½ tsp golden caster sugar,
    plus extra
    for sprinkling
30g (1¼oz) plain flour,
    sifted
1 medium egg

For the filling
100ml (4fl oz) double cream
1½ tbsp drinking
    chocolate

For the icing
40g (1½oz) golden
    icing sugar
¼ tsp Camp coffee essence

Piping bag and 1cm
    (½in) star nozzle

High Flying BOAC Hostess, Tessa Trump, was caught smuggling these lovely little mocha éclairs, light with choux pastry, topped with coffee icing and filled with chocolate cream, in her in-flight luggage. Despite her lawyer's ardent appeal for leniency, her weeping mother and the website freetessatrump.com set up by her father, she got 25 years with no parole.

★ Preheat the oven to 200°C/400°F/Gas 6 and line a baking sheet with baking parchment.

★ Slosh the milk into a small pan with the butter. Heat gently, then bring to a rolling boil and add the sugar and flour. Stir the mixture together quickly until it forms a ball. Tip the ball into a bowl to cool until just warm, then beat in the egg, slowly and surely, bit by bit, until the mixture drops off the spoon easily. You may not need to use all of the egg, so don't panic.

★ Spoon the mixture into a piping bag fitted with a 1cm (½in) round nozzle and pipe around 16 fingers, spaced well apart, on the parchment. Each finger should be about 5cm (2in) long. Bake them in the oven for 13–15 minutes. Pierce the side of each finger, and bake for 5 minutes more until cooked inside. Cool on a wire rack.

★ Make the filling by whipping the cream in a bowl until soft peaks form. Lush. Fold in the drinking chocolate. Spoon into a piping bag with a 1cm (½in) round nozzle and pipe into the middle of each éclair.

★ Sift the icing sugar into a bowl and add the Camp coffee essence. Stir in 1–2 teaspoons of boiling water. Carefully spoon the icing on top of the éclairs to cover them. Give them 20 minutes at least to set, then eat 'em.

PURVEYORS OF
HOPE
AND
GREENWOOD
SPLENDID GOODS ®

TOP-NOTCH TEA
AND T'RIFFIC
TIPPLES

GINGER CORDIAL
WITH MINT AND LEMON

★ **Makes 400ml (14fl oz) camp cordial**

★ **Takes 20 minutes to make; plus chilling, and 5 minutes to practise 'doing your best'.**

400g (14oz) golden
    granulated sugar
100g (4oz) fresh root
    ginger, grated
Juice of ½ lemon
Sparkling water, chilled,
    to dilute
Ice cubes, to serve
Sprigs of mint, to serve

Boy Scouts around the land will place a loyal hand on their woggle in praise of this refreshing ginger cordial, with a wink of lemon and a tingle of mint. After a hot summer's day Scout Leader, Bruce Woodcock, sparks up the campfire, tightens his guy ropes and strokes his 'Best Camp' badge. It's time for some toasted marshmallows, a glass of sparkling ginger ale and a bit of Ging Gang Goolie.

★ Kindly put the sugar and 200ml (7fl oz) cold water in a pan and heat gently to dissolve the sugar. Bring to the boil and simmer for 5 minutes. Top scouting effort.

★ Stir in the fresh ginger and lemon juice and simmer for a further 5 minutes then strain it into a hot, sterilised bottle and seal. Cool then chill.

★ When you are thirsty, pour a slug of cordial into a glass, top it up with sparkling water and add ice cubes and a gay sprig of fresh mint to the glass. Enjoy it, it's lovely. Store the remainder in the fridge and guzzle it within two weeks.

Sing-a-long
Ging gang goo,
ging gang goo, etc.

THAI ICED TEA

★ **Serves 4 skinnies**

★ **Takes 5 minutes to make; plus steeping, and chilling on the terrace.**

1 green tea bag
3 sticks of lemongrass, finely chopped
Ice cubes, to serve
4 slices of lime, to serve
Lime basil or regular basil sprigs, to serve

What a delightful drink this is, green tea infused with lemongrass and lime and decorated with lime basil. Green tea is truly amazing. It has special fat-busting stuff in it that boosts your doo-dah-day by 4 per cent – guaranteed to make you as thin as a Ryvita. If you have run out of green tea, you'll be delighted to learn that cream cakes do exactly the same job.

★ Boldly brew the green tea using 900ml (32fl oz) boiling water. Let it stand for 4–5 minutes before adding the lemongrass. Remove the tea bag then you may leave the tea in the fridge to chill.
★ Put two or three ice cubes into each of four glasses, then strain the tea equally among them. Plonk a slice of lime and sprig of basil in each glass. Serve immediately and just watch the blubber fall off.

SPARKLING JASMINE TEA

'Let us take a turn around the garden, sister,' says Mr Dandy to Elizabeth Bonnet. 'The night is fragrant with white jasmine flowers. See how she opens her sweet blossom to share the secrets of her perfume? Me thinks I will stuff some blooms in the valley of your magnificent orbs laters. Come let us fill a silver flask with jasmine tea, cinnamon and lemons and have a bit of a fumble in the shrubbery.'

'Wicked,' says Miss Bonnet, clocking his uncommonly tight breeches.

★ Do be so kind as to plonk the jasmine tea bags in a jug with the cinnamon stick and 300ml (10½fl oz) boiling water. Please ignore it while it brews for 4 minutes.

★ Now I'd like you to discard the tea bags and stir in the sugar. Chill the brew until nice and cold.

★ Take 4 glasses and divide the tea between them. Top up with sparkling water, or champagne if you are feeling naughty.

★ **Serves 4 admirably**

★ **Takes 10 minutes to make; plus chilling, and 45 minutes' fumbling time.**

4 Jasmine green tea bags
1 cinnamon stick
50g (2oz) Demerara sugar
Chilled sparkling water or
   champagne
4 slices of lemon

SICILIAN LEMONADE

★ **Makes 650ml (23fl oz) zingy fresh cordial**

★ **Takes 20 minutes for cook to make; plus cooling, and about an hour frolicking on the tennis court.**

400g (14oz) golden
   granulated sugar
Zest and juice of 6
   unwaxed lemons
Ice cubes, to serve
Sparkling water, chilled

Doves in the cote chuckle, heads tucked, plucking at crumbs. Daphne's open window admits a soap-soft breeze, cool on her tennis-flushed cheeks. The afternoon's sport has left her peckish and fractious.

'Golly gosh, cook has done us proud again,' says James, stretching his long limbs on the chaise longue.

'Pass the lemonade, darling,' says Daphne, keen for something sparkling, zingy and refreshing. 'Tennis can be so bothersome.'

'Double damn and blast!' cries John, as a freshly baked strawberry tart crumbles in his hand, 'Now I've dropped jam on my flip-flops.'

★ First, call cook. Ask her to put the sugar and 200ml (7fl oz) water in a pan and heat gently to dissolve the sugar. Then she must bring it up to the boil and simmer for 5 minutes until splendidly syrupy.
★ Then she should add the lemon zest and juice and simmer for another 5 minutes, before pouring it, without delay, into a hot sterilised bottle, leaving it to come to room temperature, and asking Jeeves to pop it into your refrigerator or ice house.
★ To serve, pour a good slug of cordial into a glass, add a tinkle of ice cubes and top it up with sploosh of sparkling water. You may continue to enjoy this delightful bevy for a further two weeks if you wisely store in it your new-fangled refrigerator.

RUSSIAN TEA

Alexandra and Jonty are setting out by camel caravan from China to Russia. They are well prepared for the 6000-mile journey. Alex is wearing her sunray pleated skirt, ideal for camel riding, and Jonty is wearing his hump-proof trousers. Alex has been clever enough to pack some oranges, lemons and cloves to mix with their cargo of Oolong, Keemun and Lapsang Souchong tea. It is midnight at the oasis, the campfire's whirling smoke permeates the Caravan Tea and Jonty is fantasizing about a sheik.

★ Put the sugar, orange zest and juice, lemon juice and cloves in a small pan and add 250ml (9fl oz) water. Now, slowly bring to the boil to allow the sugar to dissolve. Simmer for 5 minutes. Strain the syrup then let it cool.
★ Put the tea bags in a jug and add 900ml (32fl oz) boiling water. Leave to brew for 3–4 fragrant minutes.
★ Divide the citrus syrup between four Russian tea cups or mugs and pour over the tea. Stir, and serve as hot as the desert.

★ **Serves 4 adventurers**

★ **Takes 15 minutes to make; plus cooling, and six months to travel by camel from China to Russia.**

75g (3oz) granulated
    sugar
Zest and juice of 1 orange
Juice of 1 lemon
2 whole cloves
2–4 Russian caravan
    tea bags

BELLINI

★ **Serves 12 admirably (or 1 unwisely)**

★ **Takes 10 minutes to make, and 10 minutes to send me a letter of complaint.**

2–3 soft, ripe peaches (around 300g/12oz)
½ tsp vanilla extract
Two 75cl bottles of champagne, chilled

The Bellini was invented between 6.30pm and 7.30pm in a pub in the village of Italy by a man by the name of Harry Bellini-Cipriani. Despite being foreign, it is a blissful marriage of ripe peach flesh and shudderingly cold champagne, with a touch of vanilla. My aunty Margery was a peach fanatic and her 'whisper blush' three-piece bathroom suite, which comprised of a corner whirlpool in graduated peach tones and a rubber-backed bath mat in 'sunset boulevard', was a shrine to sophistication.

★ Cut a cross in the top and bottom of the peaches and put them in a bowl. Cover with boiling water and leave them for a minute. Drain them and peel away the skin: yes, it is hot; it has been in boiling water, this is how the world works. Chop up the peaches, throwing away the stones, and put the flesh in a mini blender with the vanilla. Whiz to make a purée. Or smash it up with a great big spoon or a brick or something. Anyway, it should end up as a purée.

★ Spoon a little purée into each champagne glass and top up with champagne. Stir the peachilisciousness to mix the purée into the fizz good and proper.

DARJEELING GIN FIZZ

In the hills of Darjeeling, the god Shiva exhales a gentle breeze across the sun-drenched valleys, the fog of his loving breath brings moisture, quenching rivers flow from his head, feeding the glorious black tea bushes. The green leaves stretch their fragrant fingers to a flush, perfect for plucking and marrying with some good gin, wedges of cool cucumber and fresh mint.

In the valleys of Sainsbury's, tanned goddess Debbie tuts at my trolley and points an orange finger to the 'baskets only' sign.

★ Please make a super-strong tea in a jug with the Darjeeling tea bags and 300ml (10½fl oz) boiling water. Leave it to steep for 5 minutes.
★ Throw away the bags and stir in the sugar until it has dissolved. Chill until perfectly cold.
★ Now tinkle two or three ice cubes into six glasses and share the Darjeeling mixture equally among them. Add the gin, chopped cucumber and mint sprigs to each glass, and top up with sparkling water.

★ **Serves 6 worthy friends**

★ **Takes 10 minutes to make; plus chilling and a lifetime to discover your inner goddess.**

3 Darjeeling tea bags
50g (2oz) caster sugar
Ice cubes, to serve
6 generous slugs of good quality gin (9 or 15 if no one is looking)
¼ cucumber, halved lengthways, seeds removed and chopped
Sprigs of mint, to garnish
Sparkling water, chilled

PROSECCO WITH NASTURTIUMS

★ **Serves 6, or 1 depending.**

★ **Takes 5 minutes to make; plus 30 minutes of fierce Zumba.**

6 edible nasturtiums
A splash of rosewater
1–2 tsp golden caster
  sugar
75cl bottle of chilled
  Prosecco

Lady Jane Clutterbuck sojourned at elegant Evermead House Hotel, Torquay, in the last summer of her golden years. It was she who invented this darling drink, a crystal-cold Prosecco with a soupçon of rosewater and a light pinch of sugar. The edible nasturtium came a little later when, after a fierce session of 'Zumba with Pauline', a dizzy spell catapulted her into a flower bed.

★ Pop a nasturtium into each of six glasses. Add a drop of rosewater and a pinch of sugar to each glass, and top them up with the chilled Prosecco. Simple but intoxicating.

EARL GREY VODKA

This famous tea was named after Earl Grey, the famous New York jazz musician. I've added the fragrant tea leaves to a bottle of vodka with a little sugar. After a three-day bender, the Earl produced some of his finest work; Gonna get along without Cha Now (Patience and Prudence), Tea-Bop-a-Lula (Gene Vincent) and Blue Suede Brews (Elvis Prezzers).

★ Do put a funnel in the top of the vodka bottle. Now break open a tea bag and pour in the tea leaves, followed by the sugar. Please screw the cap back onto the bottle and give it a good Elvis shake.

★ Kindly store the bottle in the fridge for two weeks, then strain and re-bottle it.

★ Serve the liquor over ice with a twist of lemon if you are brave, or add a single measure (25ml) to a hot cup of Earl Grey tea if the kids are misbehaving and you need to take the edge off.

★ **Makes one extremely alcoholic 75cl bottle**

★ **Takes 5 minutes to make; plus steeping, chilling and 20 minutes to polish your horn.**

75cl bottle of vodka
6g Earl Grey tea leaves (a teabag is fine)
1 tbsp golden caster sugar
Ice cubes, to serve
Strips of lemon rind, to serve (optional)

FIRESIDE RUM TEA

★ **Serves 4 admirably**

★ **Takes 5 minutes to make, and 5 minutes to polish your baubles.**

4 tbsp maple syrup
½ tsp ground cinnamon
The seeds of 1 cardamom
   pod, ground down to
   a powder in a pestle
   and mortar
4 black tea bags
100ml (4fl oz) dark rum
4 cinnamon sticks,
   to serve

Here we are in North Pole House, where it is Christmas every day. The fire pops and crackles in the grate, snow drifts silently, the great, white plains alight with ribbons of dancing northern lights.

Father Christmas is enjoying a lovely glass of Rum Tea with his pirate chum Cap'n Leadenfoot.

'Here's to adventure on high seas and a muckle of treasure!' says FC, lifting his steaming glass of rum, maple syrup, cinnamon and cardamom. 'That will put hairs on your chest!'

'Shurrup! Shirley Bassey's* on!' tuts the Cap'n, dusting mince pie from his negligee.

★ Please mix the maple syrup and spices together in a bowl. Sniff.
★ Now brew a pot of tea with the tea bags and leave to steep for 1–2 minutes – a light brew is best as it happens.
★ Divide the tea among four mugs and add a good splash of rum to each. Spoon a tablespoon of the spiced syrup into each mug, stir and serve with a cinnamon stick.

* followed by Judy Garland's Songs from Easter Parade Medley.

STOCKISTS

Some of the baking ingredients and equipment may be tricky to track down locally, but they are all available online or by phone. Failing that, give me a tinkle and I'll get dressed and pop over.

HOPE AND GREENWOOD
www.hopeandgreenwood.co.uk
Mail order: 020 8613 1777
Sugar HQ: 020 7738 2013
For all manner of sweet delights, including lemon sherbet crystals, rhubarb and custard sweets, coffee beans, toffees and toffee slab, liquorice root, chocolate truffles, 100g 73 per cent dark chocolate bars, milk and white chocolate bars. The chocolate bars are perfect for using in baking. You can visit one of our two London stores for Hope and Greenwood cookware, textiles and ceramics, or you can shop for supplies from the comfort of your nightie.

JOHN LEWIS
www.johnlewis.com
Tel: 08456 049 049
For general baking kit, a good range of kitchen scales, baking sheets, cake tins, moulds, cutters and measuring spoons.

LAKELAND
www.lakeland.co.uk
Tel: 015394 88100

For general bakeware and ingredients, a good range of piping bag kits, baking sheets, cake tins, cases and cutters and decorations.

SQUIRES
www.squires-shop.com
Tel: 0845 6171810
For foodstuffs and equipment, including edible gold leaf and a great selection of muffin cases.

For specific top-notch baking equipment:

The mini fluted deep tart tins for the Blueberry Bakewells with Lemon Syllabub and the Orange Custard Tarts are made by Kitchen Craft, and are widely available in good kitchen shops or from **www.dennyandsons.co.uk (Tel: 01379 852248).**

The shallow tart tins for the Treacle Tarts are made by Matfer and are available from **www.russums-shop.co.uk (Tel: 0845 094 2030).**

The petit four tins for the Cute Berry Tarts are available from **www.chefs.net (Tel: 0800 988 8981).**

The 9-hole cake mould for the Malt Tea Loaf made by Pavoni, is available from **www.caterfor.co.uk (Tel: 0844 736 5726).**

INDEX

THANK YOU

Thank you to all my splendid chums who made the summer of 2012 such a treat.

Teddy Fortes

Bex Ham 'n' Cheese

Lord Barnett of Cambridge

Roy the Wonderscout

Big thanks The Vintage Store in East Dulwich for putting up with me.